Twelve Old English Poems

Twelve Old English Poems

A Dual-Language Edition with Parallel Texts

MODERN ENGLISH VERSE

TRANSLATION BY

Sung-Il Lee

RESOURCE *Publications* · Eugene, Oregon

TWELVE OLD ENGLISH POEMS
A Dual-Language Edition with Parallel Texts

Resource Publications
An Imprint of Wipf and Stock Publishers
199 W. 8th Ave., Suite 3
Eugene, OR 97401

www.wipfandstock.com

PAPERBACK ISBN: 979-8-3852-4279-5
HARDCOVER ISBN: 979-8-3852-4280-1
EBOOK ISBN: 979-8-3852-4281-8

Cataloguing-in-Publication data:

Name: Lee, Sung-Il.

Title: Twelve old english poems : a dual-language edition with parallel texts / by Sung-Il Lee.

Description: Eugene, OR: Resource Publications, 2025

Identifiers: ISBN 979-8-3852-4279-5 (paperback) | ISBN 979-8-3852-4280-1 (hardcover) | ISBN 979-8-3852-4281-8 (ebook)

Subjects: LCSH: Poetry. | Poetry—English language | English poetry—Old English, ca. 450–1100—Translations into English

Classification: PN1010 L44 2025 (paperback) | PN1010 (ebook)

VERSION NUMBER 03/11/26

In memory of
Professor Robert D. Stevick

Textual Source of the Old English Poems

All the poems in Old English appearing in this anthology are from *The Anglo-Saxon Poetic Records: A Collective Edition*, published by Columbia University Press.

Dream of the Rood: Vol. II (1932), Edited by George Philip Krapp

The Wanderer: Vol. III (1936), Edited by George Philip Krapp & Elliott Van Kirk Dobbie

The Seafarer: Vol. III

The Lament of an Outcast (or *The Wife's Lament*): Vol. III

Deor: Vol. III

The Battle of Brunanburh: Vol. VI (1942), Edited by Elliott Van Kirk Dobbie

The Battle of Maldon: Vol. VI

The Battle of Finnsburh: Vol. VI

The Ruin: Vol. III

Waldere: Vol. VI

Widsith: Vol. III

The Husband's Message: Vol. III

Contents

Preface

THIS ANTHOLOGY IS MEANT to be a possible help to the students struggling to read Old English poems in their original texts. It is true that, even after taking an introductory course in Old English, one feels inadequately prepared for launching into reading poems in it. Even after studying its basic grammar, students are bound to consider Old English poetry as a mountain looming high, discouraging them from harboring thoughts of climbing it. The first step, however, has to be taken, no matter how steep and rugged the road stretching ahead may look. With the help of a guide, however, one may gradually start feeling that the tortuous lane meandering through the marshland of inflection and entangled word-order will finally be trodden and be over. This volume dares to assume the role of a guide for those willing to meet the challenge of coping with Old English poetry.

For a student of Old English poetry, having read *Beowulf* in its entirety is a consummation devoutly to be wished, for even in a graduate course devoted to the epic, shortage of time often compels an instructor to skip the passages of digression in classroom reading. Yet a certain degree of acquaintance with well-known shorter Old English poems is a must. For that reason, the poems, or fragments, contained in this volume may be covered in an introductory course in Old English.

The editorial scheme of making my translation run parallel with the original texts in Old English arose in hopes of providing ready help to the readers. While struggling with the texts in Old English, checking each word by turning to the glossaries provided by scholars, the students may wish to have their own translations reconfirmed by another's. The *en face* arrangement of the original text and its modern English translation running parallel will help the readers to feel comfortable for having their own translations confirmed by another's.

I dedicate this slim volume to the memory of Professor Robert D. Stevick, who could not see the outcome of this long-delayed project of mine I wished to have reviewed by him. (SL)

POEMS

Dream of the Rood

Hwæt! Ic swefna cyst secgan wylle,
hwæt me gemætte to midre nihte,
syðþan reordberend reste wunedon!
Þuhte me þæt ic gesawe syllicre treow
on lyft lædan, leohte bewunden,   5
beama beorhtost. Eall þæt beacen wæs
begoten mid golde. Gimmas stodon
fægere æt foldan sceatum, swylce þær fife wæron
uppe on þam eaxlegespanne. Beheoldon þær engel dryhtnes ealle,
fægere þurh forðgesceaft. Ne wæs ðær huru fracodes gealga,   10
ac hine þær beheoldon halige gastas,
men ofer moldan, ond eall þeos mære gesceaft.
Syllic wæs se sigebeam, ond ic synnum fah,
forwunded mid wommum. Geseah ic wuldres treow,
wædum geweorðode, wynnum scinan,   15
gegyred mid golde; gimmas hæfdon
bewrigene weorðlice wealdendes treow.
Hwæðre ic þurh þæt gold ongytan meahte
earmra ærgewin, þæt hit ærest ongan
swætan on þa swiðran healfe. Eall ic wæs mid sorgum gedrefed,   20
forht ic wæs for þære fægran gesyhðe. Geseah ic þæt fuse beacen
wendan wædum ond bleom; hwilum hit wæs mid wætan bestemed,
beswyled mid swates gange, hwilum mid since gegyrwed.
Hwæðre ic þær licgende lange hwile
beheold hreowcearig hælendes treow,   25
oððæt ic gehyrde þæt hit hleoðrode.
Ongan þa word sprecan wudu selesta:
"Þæt wæs geara iu, (ic þæt gyta geman),
þæt ic wæs aheawen holtes on ende,
astyred of stefne minum. Genaman me ðær strange feondas,   30
geworhton him þær to wæfersyne, heton me heora wergas hebban.

Listen! I wish to tell the best of my dreams,
What I had in the middle of the night,
While the speech-bearers remained silent!

It seemed to me that I saw a wondrous tree
Borne aloft, enwrapped in light,   5
The brightest of all the trees. The beacon was
Covered with gold entirely. Glittering gems lay
On the surface of the earth; there were also five
Upon the shoulder-beam. All the Lord's angels, beautiful by creation,
Looked on there. That was indeed not a gallows for a felon,   10
For the holy spirits looked on it there, as
Men over the earth, and all this glorious creation did.

Wonderful was the tree of triumph; and I was stained by sins,
Deeply wounded, bearing the scars of sins. I saw the tree of glory,
Adorned with glittering wear, shine beautifully,   15
Bedecked with gold; gems had
Duly covered the tree of the Lord.
Nevertheless I could perceive through that gold
The bygone strife of the miserable, see that it first began to
Bleed on the right side. I was entirely afflicted with sorrow;   20
I was frightened before the beautiful sight. I saw that hastening beacon
Change its garments and colors: at times it was bedewed with blood,
Drenched with the flow of blood; at times bedecked with treasure.

Nevertheless, lying there a long while,
I beheld the tree of the Savior in sorrow,   25
Till I heard that it spoke;
The best tree began to say these words:

"It was long ago—I still remember it—
That I was hewn down at the edge of a wood,
Taken away from my trunk. Strong-handed foes grabbed me there,   30
Made a spectacle of me for them there, asked me to heave their outlaws.

Bæron me ðær beornas on eaxlum, oððæt hie me on beorg asetton,
gefæstnodon me þær feondas genoge. Geseah ic þa frean mancynnes
efstan elne mycle þæt he me wolde on gestigan.
Þær ic þa ne dorste ofer dryhtnes word   35
bugan oððe berstan, þa ic bifian geseah
eorðan sceatas. Ealle ic mihte
feondas gefyllan, hwæðre ic fæste stod.
Ongyrede hine þa geong hæleð, (þæt wæs god ælmihtig),
strang ond stiðmod. Gestah he on gealgan heanne,   40
modig on manigra gesyhðe, þa he wolde mancyn lysan.
Bifode ic þa me se beorn ymbclypte. Ne dorste ic hwæðre bugan to eorðan,
feallan to foldan sceatum, ac ic sceolde fæste standan.
Rod wæs ic aræred. Ahof ic ricne cyning,
heofona hlaford, hyldan me ne dorste.   45
Þurhdrifan hi me mid deorcan næglum. On me syndon þa dolg gesiene,
opene inwidhlemmas. Ne dorste ic hira nænigum sceððan.
Bysmeredon hie unc butu ætgædere. Eall ic wæs mid blode bestemed,
begoten of þæs guman sidan, siððan he hæfde his gast onsended.
Feala ic on þam beorge gebiden hæbbe   50
wraðra wyrda. Geseah ic weruda god
þearle þenian. Þystro hæfdon
bewrigen mid wolcnum wealdendes hræw,
scirne sciman, sceadu forðeode,
wann under wolcnum. Weop eal gesceaft,   55
cwiðdon cyninges fyll. Crist wæs on rode.
Hwæðere þær fuse feorran cwoman
to þam æðelinge. Ic þæt eall beheold.
Sare ic wæs mid sorgum gedrefed, hnag ic hwæðre þam secgum to handa,
eaðmod elne mycle. Genamon hie þær ælmihtigne god,   60
ahofon hine of ðam hefian wite. Forleton me þa hilderincas
standan steame bedrifenne; eall ic wæs mid strælum forwundod.
Aledon hie ðær limwerigne, gestodon him æt his lices heafdum,
beheoldon hie ðær heofenes dryhten, ond he hine ðær hwile reste,
meðe æfter ðam miclan gewinne. Ongunnon him þa moldern wyrcan   65

4

People bore me there on their shoulders, till they set me up on a hill;
Many enemies fastened me there. Then I saw the Lord of mankind
Hasten with great zeal, for He wished to mount on me.
There I did not dare then, against the Lord's word,   35
Bend or burst, when I saw the surface
Of the earth tremble. I could have crushed
All my enemies; nevertheless I stood fast.
  "Then the young Hero took off his clothes—that was God Almighty—
Strong and resolute; he mounted on the tall cross,   40
Brave in many people's view, as he would redeem mankind.
I trembled when the Man embraced me; yet I did not dare to bend to earth,
Fall to the surface of the earth, but I had to stand fast.
I was raised to be the Rood; I heaved the powerful King,
Lord of the heavens. I did not dare to bow down.   45
  "They pierced me with dark nails; on me are the wounds seen,
Open, malicious wounds; nor did I dare to injure any of them.
They mocked us both together. I was entirely soaked in blood,
Drenched, from the Man's side, when he had his spirit sent forth.
  "Upon the hill I have endured many   50
Of the cruel fates: I saw the God of the multitudes
Stretched out painfully. The shades of night had
Covered with clouds the body of the Lord,
The shining splendor; a shadow went forth,
Black beneath the clouds. All creation wept,   55
Bewailed the King's death, for Christ was on the cross.
  "However, there came the eager ones in haste from afar
To the Prince; I beheld that all. I was in pain,
Afflicted with sorrow; I stooped, however, to the hands of the men,
Humble, with great zeal. There they laid hold of Almighty God,   60
Heaved Him from the heavy torment; the battle-brave ones left me
Standing covered with blood; I was all wounded with arrows.
There they laid down the limb-weary one, stood at His body's head;
They beheld there the Lord of Heaven, and He rested there awhile,
Weary after the great struggle. Then they began to build a tomb for Him, 65

beornas on banan gesyhðe; curfon hie ðæt of beorhtan stane,
gesetton hie ðæron sigora wealdend. Ongunnon him þa sorhleoð galan
earme on þa æfentide, þa hie woldon eft siðian,
meðe fram þam mæran þeodne. Reste he ðær mæte weorode.

Hwæðere we ðær greotende gode hwile   70
stodon on staðole, syððan stefn up gewat
hilderinca. Hræw colode,
fæger feorgbold. Þa us man fyllan ongan
ealle to eorðan. Þæt wæs egeslic wyrd!
Bedealf us man on deopan seaþe. Hwæðre me þær dryhtnes þegnas,   75
freondas gefrunon,
ond gyredon me golde ond seolfre.

Nu ðu miht gehyran, hæleð min se leofa,
þæt ic bealuwara weorc gebiden hæbbe,
sarra sorga. Is nu sæl cumen   80
þæt me weorðiað wide ond side
menn ofer moldan, ond eall þeos mære gesceaft,
gebiddaþ him to þyssum beacne. On me bearn godes
þrowode hwile. Forþan ic þrymfæst nu
hlifige under heofenum, ond ic hælan mæg   85
æghwylcne anra, þara þe him bið egesa to me.
Iu ic wæs geworden wita heardost,
leodum laðost, ærþan ic him lifes weg
rihtne gerymde, reordberendum.
Hwæt, me þa geweorðode wuldres ealdor   90
ofer holmwudu, heofonrices weard!
Swylce swa he his modor eac, Marian sylfe,
ælmihtig god for ealle menn
geweorðode ofer eall wifa cynn.

    Nu ic þe hate, hæleð min se leofa,   95
þæt ðu þas gesyhðe secge mannum,
onwreoh wordum þæt hit is wuldres beam,
se ðe ælmihtig god on þrowode
for mancynnes manegum synnum

The men did, in His slayer's sight; they delved it out of bright stone.
They placed therein the Lord of victories. Then they began to sing Him a dirge,
The miserable ones, in the eventide, when they would travel back,
Weary, from the glorious Prince. He rested there with no company.

"Nevertheless we stood there for a good while,   70
Weeping, on our foundation, after the voice of
The warriors faded away. The body grew cold,
The fair life's dwelling. Then a man began to lay low
All to the ground; that was a dreadful doom!
A man buried us in a deep pit. Yet the Lord's thanes, His friends,   75
Found me out there; [then they lifted me from the earth],
And they decked me with gold and silver.

"Now you can hear, my dear man,
That I have endured what the evil-doers did,
Work of painful sorrows. Now is the time come   80
That they honor me far and wide—
Men over the earth, and all this glorious creation—
Pray to this beacon. On me the Son of God
Suffered awhile; therefore, I now stand high
Glorious under the heavens, and I can save   85
Every one of those, in whom there is fear of me.

"Long ago I had become the hardest of torments,
Most loathsome to people, till I prepared for them,
For the bearers of speech, the right way of life.
Yes, Lord of glory, Guardian of the heavenly kingdom,   90
Exalted me above all the trees in the forest,
Just as He, Almighty God,
Also honored His mother, Maria herself,
For all men, well above all womanhood.

"Now I command you, my dear man,   95
That you tell this vision to other men,
Reveal in words that it is the tree of glory,
On which Almighty God suffered
For the many sins of mankind

ond Adomes ealdgewyrhtum.   100
Deað he þær byrigde, hwæðere eft dryhten aras
mid his miclan mihte mannum to helpe.
He ða on heofenas astag. Hider eft fundaþ
on þysne middangeard mancynn secan
on domdæge dryhten sylfa,   105
ælmihtig god, ond his englas mid,
þæt he þonne wile deman, se ah domes geweald,
anra gehwylcum swa he him ærur her
on þyssum lænum life geearnaþ.
Ne mæg þær ænig unforht wesan   110
for þam worde þe se wealdend cwyð.
Frineð he for þære mænige hwær se man sie,
se ðe for dryhtnes naman deaðes wolde
biteres onbyrigan, swa he ær on ðam beame dyde.
Ac hie þonne forhtiað, ond fea þencaþ   115
hwæt hie to Criste cweðan onginnen.
Ne þearf ðær þonne ænig anforht wesan
þe him ær in breostum bereð beacna selest,
ac ðurh ða rode sceal rice gesecan
of eorðwege æghwylc sawl,   120
seo þe mid wealdende wunian þenceð."
    Gebæd ic me þa to þan beame bliðe mode,
elne mycle, þær ic ana wæs
mæte werede. Wæs modsefa
afysed on forðwege, feala ealra gebad   125
langunghwila. Is me nu lifes hyht
þæt ic þone sigebeam secan mote
ana oftor þonne ealle men,
well weorþian. Me is willa to ðam
mycel on mode, ond min mundbyrd is   130
geriht to þære rode. Nah ic ricra feala
freonda on foldan, ac hie forð heonon
gewiton of worulde dreamum, sohton him wuldres cyning,

And Adam's deeds of old.   100
He tasted death there; yet the Lord rose up again
With His mighty power as help for men.
Then He ascended to the heavens. Here will come again
Onto this middle-earth to seek mankind
On Doomsday, the Lord Himself,   105
Almighty God, and His angels with Him,
That He then may judge—He has the power of doom—
Every one, according as he till then here
In this fleeting life will have earned.
No one there can be free from fear   110
For the word that the Lord will say:
He will ask before the many where the man is,
The one who in the Lord's name would taste
Of bitter death, as He before on the cross did.
But they will be afraid then, and will little think   115
What they may undertake to say to Christ.
No one then has any need there to be terrified,
Who will bear before in his breast the best beacon;
But through the rood he must seek the kingdom
Away from earth-way—each soul must—   120
That thinks of dwelling with the Eternal Lord."
     Then I prayed to the cross in glad cheer,
With great zeal, where I was alone,
With no company. My soul was
Urged on forth away; I endured many bouts   125
Of longing. Now for me life is hopeful,
That I may be able to seek the tree of victory
Alone, oftener than all the other men,
To honor it well. For me the will to do so
Is great in my mind, and my protection is   130
To be sought in the rood. I have not many powerful
Friends on earth, for they have departed hence
Forth from the joys of the world, have sought the King of glory,

9

lifiaþ nu on heofenum mid heahfædere,
wuniaþ on wuldre, ond ic wene me
daga gehwylce hwænne me dryhtnes rod,
þe ic her on eorðan ær sceawode,
on þysson lænan life gefetige
ond me þonne gebringe þær is blis mycel,
dream on heofonum, þær is dryhtnes folc
geseted to symle, þær is singal blis,
ond me þonne asette þær ic syþþan mot
wunian on wuldre, well mid þam halgum
dreames brucan. Si me dryhten freond,
se ðe her on eorþan ær þrowode
on þam gealgtreowe for guman synnum.
He us onlysde ond us lif forgeaf,
heofonlicne ham. Hiht wæs geniwad
mid bledum ond mid blisse þam þe þær bryne þolodan.
Se sunu wæs sigorfæst on þam siðfate,
mihtig ond spedig, þa he mid manigeo com,
gasta weorode, on godes rice,
anwealda ælmihtig, englum to blisse
ond eallum ðam halgum þam þe on heofonum ær
wunedon on wuldre, þa heora wealdend cwom,
ælmihtig god, þær his eðel wæs.

135

140

145

150

155

Live now in heaven with the High Father,
And dwell in glory; and I look forward to,   135
Day after day, the time when the rood of the Lord,
Which I here on earth have once looked on
In this fleeting life, will carry me off,
And then bring me where there is great bliss,
Joy in the heavens, where the Lord's people are   140
Seated at banquet, where there is perpetual bliss,
And then will set me where I may afterwards
Dwell in glory, well with the holy ones
Brook joy. May the Lord be a friend for me—
He who here on earth has once suffered   145
Upon the gallows-tree for the sins of man;
He redeemed us, and gave us life
And home heavenly. Hope was renewed with glory
And bliss, for those who had suffered the fire there.
The Son was victorious in that journey,   150
Mighty and successful, when He with many,
With a host of spirits, came into God's kingdom—
The Almighty Lord—as a blessing to the angels
And all the holy ones, who had dwelt in heaven
Already in glory, when their Lord came,   155
The Almighty God, where His home was.

The Wanderer

Oft him anhaga are gebideð,
metudes miltse, þeah þe he modcearig
geond lagulade longe sceolde
hreran mid hondum hrimcealde sæ,
wadan wræclastas. Wyrd bið ful aræd!   5
  Swa cwæð eardstapa, earfeþa gemyndig,
wraþra wælsleahta, winemæga hryre:
"Oft ic sceolde ana uhtna gehwylce
mine ceare cwiþan. Nis nu cwicra nan
þe ic him modsefan minne durre   10
sweotule asecgan. Ic to soþe wat
þæt biþ in eorle indryhten þeaw,
þæt he his ferðlocan fæste binde,
healde his hordcofan, hycge swa he wille.
Ne mæg werig mod wyrde wiðstondan,   15
ne se hreo hyge helpe gefremman.
Forðon domgeorne dreorigne oft
in hyra breostcofan bindað fæste;
swa ic modsefan minne sceolde,
oft earmcearig, eðle bidæled,   20
freomægum feor feterum sælan,
siþþan geara iu goldwine minne
hrusan heolstre biwrah, ond ic hean þonan
wod wintercearig ofer waþema gebind,
sohte sele dreorig sinces bryttan,   25
hwær ic feor oþþe neah findan meahte
þone þe in meoduhealle min mine wisse,
oþþe mec freondleasne frefran wolde,
weman mid wynnum. Wat se þe cunnað,
hu sliþen bið sorg to geferan,   30
þam þe him lyt hafað leofra geholena.

12

The solitary one often longs for mercy,
The Lord's grace, though he, sorrowful of heart,
Was long bound to stir with his hands
The rime-cold sea over the stretch of waves,
And tread the paths of exile. Fate is inexorable, indeed!   5
    So spoke the wanderer, recalling his ordeals,
Ruthless slaughters, and dear kinsmen's deaths:
"Often before the daybreak I alone had to
Bewail my care. Now there is none alive
To whom I may dare my heart   10
Clearly reveal. I know, in truth,
That it is a noble practice for a man
To lock fast his heart's coffer,
Hold his heart, and resolve as he would.
Neither can a forlorn mind withstand Fate,   15
Nor can the fierce heart be of any help.
Therefore, those eager for fame often keep
Their sadness firmly locked in their breast-chamber,
As I had to bind my heart with fetters,
Often full of care, bereft of home,   20
Removed far away from my free kinsmen.
Since long ago the darkness of earth enwrapped
My treasure-giver, and I, abject and careworn,
Drifted thence over the commingling of the waves,
And sought the hall of a treasure dispenser,   25
Where I, far or near, might come upon
The man who, in a mead-hall, would know my mind,
Or would comfort me, deprived of friends,
And entertain with delight. He who has experience
Knows what a grim companion sorrow is   30
For him that has no lord dear to him left.

Warað hine wræclast, nales wunden gold,
ferðloca freorig, nalæs foldan blæd.
Gemon he selesecgas ond sincþege,
hu hine on geoguðe his goldwine   35
wenede to wiste. Wyn eal gedreas!
    Forþon wat se þe sceal his winedryhtnes
leofes larcwidum longe forþolian,
ðonne sorg ond slæp somod ætgædre
earmne anhogan oft gebindað.   40
Þinceð him on mode þæt he his mondryhten
clyppe ond cysse, ond on cneo lecge
honda ond heafod, swa he hwilum ær
in geardagum giefstolas breac.
    Ðonne onwæcneð eft wineleas guma,   45
gesihð him biforan fealwe wegas,
baþian brimfuglas, brædan feþra,
hreosan hrim ond snaw, hagle gemenged.
    Þonne beoð þy hefigran heortan benne,
sare æfter swæsne. Sorg bið geniwad,   50
þonne maga gemynd mod geondhweorfeð;
greteð gliwstafum, georne geondsceawað
secga geseldan. Swimmað eft on weg!
Fleotendra ferð no þær fela bringeð
cuðra cwidegiedda. Cearo bið geniwad   55
þam þe sendan sceal swiþe geneahhe
ofer waþema gebind werigne sefan.
    Forþon ic geþencan ne mæg geond þas woruld
for hwan modsefa min ne gesweorce,
þonne ic eorla lif eal geondþence,   60
hu hi færlice flet ofgeafon,
modge maguþegnas. Swa þes middangeard
ealra dogra gehwam dreoseð ond falleþ,
forþon ne mæg weorþan wis wer, ær he age
wintra dæl in woruldrice. Wita sceal geþyldig,   65

Exile attends him, not brandished gold;
Cold heart follows him, not the glory of his land.
He recalls the hall-thanes and the ring receiving—
How in his youth his treasure-giver at feast   35
Used to entertain him. All joy has perished.
    Therefore, he who must long miss
The admonitions of his dear friendly lord
Knows that sorrow and sleep mingled together
Often bind a dejected wayfarer.   40
In his thought he feels as if his liege lord
He hugs and kisses, and on his knees he lays
His hands and head, as he once enjoyed
Being in the royal presence in the days gone by.
Then he awakes again a friendless man;   45
He sees before him the dark waves,
The seabirds bathe and spread their feathers,
And hoarfrost and snow mingled with hail fall.
    Then by this the wounds of heart become heavier,
Grieving after the beloved. Sorrow is renewed,   50
When memory of kinsmen traverses his mind.
He greets them joyfully, and eagerly looks around on
The warrior hall-companions; again they fleet away.
The spirits of the fleeing ones do not bring there
Many accustomed utterances. Care is renewed   55
To him, who must much too often send away
Over the commingling waves the weary spirit.
    Therefore, I cannot think upon this world
Wherefore my heart may not become dark,
When I reflect on all the life of men—   60
How they, the brave thanes, suddenly gave up
The hall-floor. So this middle-earth
Day after day falls to decay and perishes;
Therefore, a man cannot become wise, till he has lived
Enough winters in the world. A wise man must be patient,   65

ne sceal no to hatheort ne to hrædwyrde,
ne to wac wiga ne to wanhydig,
ne to forht ne to fægen, ne to feohgifre
ne næfre gielpes to georn, ær he geare cunne.
Beorn sceal gebidan, þonne he beot spriceð,   70
oþþæt collenferð cunne gearwe
hwider hreþra gehygd hweorfan wille.
Ongietan sceal gleaw hæle hu gæstlic bið,
þonne ealre þisse worulde wela weste stondeð,
swa nu missenlice geond þisne middangeard   75
winde biwaune weallas stondaþ,
hrime bihrorene, hryðge þa ederas.
Woriað þa winsalo, waldend licgað
dreame bidrorene, duguþ eal gecrong,
wlonc bi wealle. Sume wig fornom,   80
ferede in forðwege, sumne fugel oþbær
ofer heanne holm, sumne se hara wulf
deaðe gedælde, sumne dreorighleor
in eorðscræfe eorl gehydde.
Yþde swa þisne eardgeard ælda scyppend   85
oþþæt burgwara breahtma lease
eald enta geweorc idlu stodon.
     Se þonne þisne wealsteal wise geþohte
ond þis deorce lif deope geondþenceð,
frod in ferðe, feor oft gemon   90
wælsleahta worn, ond þas word acwið:
"Hwær cwom mearg? Hwær cwom mago? Hwær cwom maþþumgyfa?
Hwær cwom symbla gesetu? Hwær sindon seledreamas?
Eala beorht bune! Eala byrnwiga!
Eala þeodnes þrym! Hu seo þrag gewat,   95
genap under nihthelm, swa heo no wære.
Stondeð nu on laste leofre duguþe
weal wundrum heah, wyrmlicum fah.
Eorlas fornoman asca þryþe,

16

Must not be too hot-hearted, nor too rash in speech,
Nor be too lenient, nor too heedless,
Nor too timid, nor too easy-going, nor too greedy,
Nor ever too eager to boast, till he knows he can.
A man must wait, when he utters a boast, 70
Till he, proud-minded, knows well
To which direction the listeners' mind would move.
A wise man must understand how terrible it is,
When all the weal of this world stands waste,
As now unstable throughout this middle-earth 75
The walls stand blown upon by the wind,
Covered by hoarfrost, the dwellings storm-beaten.
The wine-halls crumble, the lords lie
Deprived of mirth; the proud host of retainers
Fell by the wall. War destroyed some of those, 80
Carried into death; a bird bore some away
Over the high sea; some a hoary wolf
Tore to death; some with sad face
Their chieftain buried in earth-cave.
The Creator of men thus laid waste this world, 85
Till what swarmed a town, bereft of mirth,
Have come to stand idle—the old works of the giants.
    He then, immersed in wise thought, reflects
Deeply on this wall-place and this dark life.
Well ripe in heart, he often calls to mind 90
The innumerable slaughters, and utters these words:
"Where did the horse go? Where the man? Where the ring-giver?
Where are the banquet-seats? Where the joys of the hall?
Alas, the bright cup! Alas, the mailed warrior!
Alas, the glory of a king! How the time fled, 95
Darkened in the nightshade, as if it had never been!
Now stands, after the dear host is gone,
A wall wondrously high, engraved with writhing dragons.
The might of spears overpowered the earls,

wæpen wælgifru, wyrd seo mære,   100
ond þas stanhleoþu stormas cnyssað,
hrið hreosende hrusan bindeð,
wintres woma, þonne won cymeð,
nipeð nihtscua, norþan onsendeð
hreo hæglfare hæleþum on andan.   105
Eal is earfoðlic eorþan rice,
onwendeð wyrda gesceaft weoruld under heofonum.
Her bið feoh læne, her bið freond læne,
her bið mon læne, her bið mæg læne,
eal þis eorþan gesteal idel weorþeð!"   110
   Swa cwæð snottor on mode, gesæt him sundor æt rune.
Til biþ se þe his treowe gehealdeþ, ne sceal næfre his torn to rycene
beorn of his breostum acyþan, nemþe he ær þa bote cunne,
eorl mid elne gefremman. Wel bið þam þe him are seceð,
frofre to fæder on heofonum, þær us eal seo fæstnung stondeð.   115

Weapons greedy for slaughter, and the unconquerable Fate.   100
And the storms beat the stony declivities,
The falling snowstorm binds the earth,
The terror of winter; then darkness comes,
The night-shadow grows dark; from the north
Blows a fierce hailstorm to chastise men.   105
All is hardship-filled in earthly kingdom,
And Fate's decree overturns the world under the heavens.
Here riches are fleeting, here a friend fleeting,
Here a man is fleeting, here a kinsman fleeting;
All this world's foundation becomes futile!"   110
      So spoke the wise man, and sat apart in meditation.
Good is he who holds his pledge: a man must never too hastily release
His indignation out of his breast, unless he knows beforehand the remedy
A man can perform with fortitude. Well is it for him who seeks mercy
                                                          for himself,
Comfort from Father in the heavens, where stands security for us all. 115

The Seafarer

Mæg ic be me sylfum soðgied wrecan,
siþas secgan, hu ic geswincdagum
earfoðhwile oft þrowade,
bitre breostceare gebiden hæbbe,
gecunnad in ceole cearselda fela, 5
atol yþa gewealc, þær mec oft bigeat
nearo nihtwaco æt nacan stefnan,
þonne he be clifum cnossað. Calde geþrungen
wæron mine fet, forste gebunden,
caldum clommum, þær þa ceare seofedun 10
hat ymb heortan; hungor innan slat
merewerges mod. Þæt se mon ne wat
þe him on foldan fægrost limpeð,
hu ic earmcearig iscealdne sæ
winter wunade wræccan lastum, 15
winemægum bidroren,
bihongen hrimgicelum; hægl scurum fleag.
Þær ic ne gehyrde butan hlimman sæ,
iscaldne wæg. Hwilum ylfete song
dyde ic me to gomene, ganetes hleoþor 20
ond huilpan sweg fore hleahtor wera,
mæw singende fore medodrince.
Stormas þær stanclifu beotan, þær him stearn oncwæð
isigfeþera; ful oft þæt earn bigeal,
urigfeþra; ne ænig hleomæga 25
feasceaftig ferð frefran meahte.
   Forþon him gelyfeð lyt, se þe ah lifes wyn
gebiden in burgum, bealosiþa hwon,
wlonc ond wingal, hu ic werig oft
in brimlade bidan sceolde. 30
Nap nihtscua, norþan sniwde,

I can compose a truthful song about myself,
Tell of the journeys—how I oftentimes have endured
Hardship through the days of toil, and
Have suffered bitter care in my heart,
Experiencing many a sorrowful abode on a boat,   5
The dreadful tossing of the waves, when it was my lot
To keep strict night-watch at the prow,
While it beat on the cliffs. My feet
Were pinched with cold, bound by the frost
With cold fetters, when hot sigh poured out   10
From my care-ridden heart. Hunger within tore
The soul of the sea-weary one. One who has chanced
To meet the fairest lot on land does not know
How I, sadly careworn, dwelt on the ice-cold sea
For a winter, on the tracks of exile,   15
Deprived of dear kinsmen, draped with frost-icicles,
While stormy hail flew. There all I could hear
Was the roaring sea, the ice-cold wave.
At times I took the song of a swan as
A source of merriment, the sound of a sea-bird,   20
The shriek of a curlew, as men's laughter,
The seagull's song as the noise in a mead-hall.
There storms beat the stone-cliff, where an icy-feathered tern
Answered them. Every once in a while an eagle screamed,
With its feathers all drenched. There was no dear kinsman   25
Who could lift me from the marsh of desolation.
   Therefore, one who is blessed with the joy of life
And has undergone few woeful occasions in towns,
Haughty and wine-flushed, will hardly guess how I,
Though weary, had to drift on the sea.   30
Night-shadow grew dark, snow blew from the north,

hrim hrusan bond, hægl feol on eorþan,
corna caldast. Forþon cnyssað nu
heortan geþohtas, þæt ic hean streamas,
sealtyþa gelac sylf cunnige; 35
monað modes lust mæla gehwylce
ferð to feran, þæt ic feor heonan
elþeodigra eard gesece.
Forþon nis þæs modwlonc mon ofer eorþan,
ne his gifena þæs god, ne in geoguþe to þæs hwæt, 40
ne in his dædum to þæs deor, ne him his dryhten to þæs hold,
þæt he a his sæfore sorge næbbe,
to hwon hine dryhten gedon wille.
Ne biþ him to hearpan hyge ne to hringþege,
ne to wife wyn ne to worulde hyht, 45
ne ymbe owiht elles, nefne ymb yða gewealc,
ac a hafað longunge se þe on lagu fundað.
Bearwas blostmum nimað, byrig fægriað,
wongas wlitigiað, woruld onetteð;
ealle þa gemoniað modes fusne 50
sefan to siþe, þam þe swa þenceð
on flodwegas feor gewitan.
Swylce geac monað geomran reorde,
singeð sumeres weard, sorge beodeð
bitter in breosthord. Þæt se beorn ne wat, 55
esteadig secg, hwæt þa sume dreogað
þe þa wræclastas widost lecgað.
    Forþon nu min hyge hweorfeð ofer hreþerlocan,
min modsefa mid mereflode
ofer hwæles eþel hweorfeð wide, 60
eorþan sceatas, cymeð eft to me
gifre ond grædig, gielleð anfloga,
hweteð on hwælweg hreþer unwearnum
ofer holma gelagu. Forþon me hatran sind
dryhtnes dreamas þonne þis deade lif, 65

22

Frost bound the ground, hail fell on the earth,
The coldest of grains. Therefore, the thoughts beat
Against my heart now—that I myself should try
The high seas, the commotion of the salt-waves.   35
My heart's desire, on every occasion, urges
My spirit to journey—that I seek
A foreign land far from here. Indeed,
There is none on earth with such a proud spirit,
With such plenteous gifts, such youthful valor,   40
So bold in his deeds, so blessed with the Lord's grace—
As not to feel anxiety about his seafaring,
About what the Lord has in store for his journey.
For him there will not be a thought of the harp nor of ring-receiving,
Nor of delight in a woman, nor of worldly hope,   45
Nor on anything else than the tossing of the waves.
But he who sets out on the water will always harbor longing.
Groves will bear blossoms, towns will prosper,
Fields will turn beautiful, the world will move along fast.
All these will impel to a voyage   50
The eager soul of one who thus contemplates on
Departing for a distant place over the foamy roads.
Thus the cuckoo urges with sad voice,
The guard of summer sings, announces sorrow
Bitter in the breast-hoard. A man in prosperity   55
Does not know what is the lot of those
Who must widely spread their paths of exile.
        Therefore, my thought now drifts over my heart's lock—
My mind ranges with the sea-waves
Over the realm of the whales, far beyond   60
The confines of the earth, coming back upon me
Anxious and eager. The lone bird shrieks,
Pulling my heart irresistibly to the sea
Over the expanse of the water. Therefore, my zeal
For the bliss in the Lord's bosom is stronger than for this life, 65

læne on londe. Ic gelyfe no
þæt him eorðwelan ece stondað.
Simle þreora sum þinga gehwylce,
ær his tid aga, to tweon weorþeð;
adl oþþe yldo oþþe ecghete   70
fægum fromweardum feorh oðþringeð.
Forþon þæt bið eorla gehwam æftercweþendra
lof lifgendra lastworda betst,
þæt he gewyrce, ær he on weg scyle,
fremum on foldan wið feonda niþ,   75
deorum dædum deofle togeanes,
þæt hine ælda bearn æfter hergen,
ond his lof siþþan lifge mid englum
awa to ealdre, ecan lifes blæd,
dream mid dugeþum. Dagas sind gewitene,   80
ealle onmedlan eorþan rices;
næron nu cyningas ne caseras
ne goldgiefan swylce iu wæron,
þonne hi mæst mid him mærþa gefremedon
ond on dryhtlicestum dome lifdon.   85
Gedroren is þeos duguð eal, dreamas sind gewitene,
wuniað þa wacran ond þas woruld healdaþ,
brucað þurh bisgo. Blæd is gehnæged,
eorþan indryhto ealdað ond searað,
swa nu monna gehwylc geond middangeard.   90
Yldo him on fareð, onsyn blacað,
gomelfeax gornað, wat his iuwine,
æþelinga bearn, eorþan forgiefene.
Ne mæg him þonne se flæschoma, þonne him þæt feorg losað,
ne swete forswelgan ne sar gefelan,   95
ne hond onhreran ne mid hyge þencan.
Þeah þe græf wille golde stregan
broþor his geborenum, byrgan be deadum,
maþmum mislicum þæt hine mid wille,

Bleak and fleeting on the earth. I do not believe
That the worldly weal lasts for ever.
Always one of the three things, without exception,
Will cast doubt before one reaches his life's end.
Illness or old age or war is bound 70
To deprive a doomed man of his life.
Therefore, the ultimate fame for every man
Is the praise of the living and speaking after.
Thus, before he goes away, he must act through
Good deeds on earth to incur the enmity of the fiends, 75
Through bold deeds against the devil's wish,
So that the children of men may praise him afterwards,
And love for him may live on among the angels
For ever and ever—the glory of eternal life,
Joy among the heavenly hosts. The days are gone, 80
Along with all the pomp of the earthly kingdom.
There have not been lately kings nor emperors
Nor gold-givers such as formerly were,
When they performed the most glorious deeds
And lived in the most lordly glory. 85
All this clan is fallen apart, the joys are no more.
Only the weaklings live on and hold the world,
Occupied in petty labor. Glory is diminished;
Earthly honor fades and withers away,
As each of the men all over the earth does now. 90
Old age comes upon him, his face turns pale;
The gray-haired grieves, recalling his former friends,
The princes' sons, now committed to clay.
When life is lost, then one's body can
Neither swallow sweets, nor feel sore, 95
Nor move his hands, nor think in mind.
Though a brother may wish to strew gold on a grave
For his departed brother, bury many a treasure
Along to accompany him in his journey,

ne mæg þære sawle þe biþ synna ful   100
gold to geoce for godes egsan,
þonne he hit ær hydeð þenden he her leofað.

   Micel biþ se meotudes egsa, forþon hi seo molde oncyrreð;
se gestaþelade stiþe grundas,
eorþan sceatas ond uprodor.   105
Dol bið se þe him his dryhten ne ondrædeþ; cymeð him se deað unþinged.
Eadig bið se þe eaþmod leofaþ; cymeð him seo ar of heofonum,
meotod him þæt mod gestaþelað, forþon he in his meahte gelyfeð.
Stieran mon sceal strongum mode, ond þæt on staþelum healdan,
ond gewis werum, wisum clæne,   110
scyle monna gehwylc mid gemete healdan
wiþ leofne ond wiþ laþne *   *   * bealo,
þeah þe he hine wille fyres fulne *   *   *
oþþe on bæle forbærnedne
his geworhtne wine. Wyrd biþ swiþre,   115
meotud meahtigra þonne ænges monnes gehygd.
   Uton we hycgan hwær we ham agen,
ond þonne geþencan hu we þider cumen,
ond we þonne eac tilien, þæt we to moten
in þa ecan eadignesse,   120
þær is lif gelong in lufan dryhtnes,
hyht in heofonum. Þæs sy þam halgan þonc,
þæt he usic geweorþade, wuldres ealdor,
ece dryhten, in ealle tid. Amen.

Gold cannot be of help against the terror of God   100
For the soul that is full of sins,
Though he hides it before while he lives here.
    Great is the fear of God, for which the earth evolves:
He established firm grounds,
The surface of the earth and the sky above.   105
Foolish is he who dreads not his Lord; unforeseen death will come to him.
Blessed is he who lives in humility; heavenly grace will come to him.
God will make that spirit firm for him, because he believes in His might.
Man must suppress violent mood, and hold it in confinement,
And be trustworthy to men, clean in his ways.   110
Each man must hold in measure. . . .
. . . . harm against a beloved and against a loathed,
Though he may wish him full of fire. . . .
Or he may wish his new-gotten friend
Burnt in fire. Fate is more powerful,   115
God mightier, than any man can conceive.
Let us consider where our home is,
And then think how we may go there.
And then we may also strive to go there—
Into the everlasting bliss,   120
Where life depends on the love of God,
Hope in heaven. Thanks be to the Holy One for this—
That He, the Father of glory, the eternal Lord,
Lifted us up in all time. Amen.

The Lament of an Outcast [or, The Wife's Lament]

"Ic þis giedd wrece bi me ful geomorre,
minre sylfre sið. Ic þæt secgan mæg,
hwæt ic yrmþa gebad, siþþan ic up weox,
niwes oþþe ealdes, no ma þonne nu.
A ic wite wonn minra wræcsiþa.   5
  "Ærest min hlaford gewat heonan of leodum
ofer yþa gelac; hæfde ic uhtceare
hwær min leodfruma londes wære.
Ða ic me feran gewat folgað secan,
wineleas wræcca, for minre weaþearfe.   10
Ongunnon þæt þæs monnes magas hycgan
þurh dyrne geþoht, þæt hy todælden unc,
þæt wit gewidost in woruldrice
lifdon laðlicost, ond mec longade.
Het mec hlaford min herheard niman,   15
ahte ic leofra lyt on þissum londstede,
holdra freonda. Forþon is min hyge geomor,
ða ic me ful gemæcne monnan funde,
heardsæligne, hygegeomorne,
mod miþendne, morþor hycgendne.   20
Bliþe gebæro ful oft wit beotedan
þæt unc ne gedælde nemne deað ana
owiht elles; eft is þæt onhworfen,
is nu * * * swa hit no wære
freondscipe uncer. Sceal ic feor ge neah   25
mines felaleofan fæhðu dreogan.
  "Heht mec mon wunian on wuda bearwe,
under actreo in þam eorðscræfe.
Eald is þes eorðsele, eal ic eom oflongad,
sindon dena dimme, duna uphea,   30
bitre burgtunas, brerum beweaxne,

"I sing this song about myself in deep sorrow
By telling what I have undergone. I truthfully can say
What misery I have gone through since I grew up—
Whether lately or in the days long gone, never more than now.
I have always suffered the torment of living in exile.   5
    "First, my lord departed hence from his people
Over the turbulent wave; at each dawn I grieved,
Wondering where my lord on earth would be.
Then I, a forlorn wretch, unable to bear my woe,
Set out on a journey in search of my service.   10
My man's kinsfolk began to conspire
In a dark plan to separate us two,
So that we would be far apart in this world
And live in great misery—and my heart ached.
My lord ordered me to dwell here;   15
I have none of my dear ones, in this part of the world,
Not one of my faithful friends. So my heart is heavy
To perceive that the man most companionable to me,
Stricken by ill luck, sad in heart,
Hiding his deep thought, even contemplates my death.   20
Joyfully we would often swear
That nothing but death would sever us two;
All that has turned the other way round;
It is now as if it had never been—
Love of ours. Far and near must I endure   25
The hatred my dear man harbors toward me.
    "He ordered me to dwell in a wood grove,
Under an oak tree, in a cave dug in the earth.
Old is the earth-hall; I am so pressed by longing.
The valleys are dark, the hills steep and high,   30
The hedges are sharp, overgrown with briars—

wic wynna leas. Ful oft mec her wraþe begeat
fromsiþ frean. Frynd sind on eorþan,
leofe lifgende, leger weardiað,
þonne ic on uhtan ana gonge   35
under actreo geond þas eorðscrafu.
Þær ic sittan mot sumorlangne dæg,
þær ic wepan mæg mine wræcsiþas,
earfoþa fela; forþon ic æfre ne mæg
þære modceare minre gerestan,   40
ne ealles þæs longaþes þe mec on þissum life begeat."

   A scyle geong mon wesan geomormod,
heard heortan geþoht, swylce habban sceal
bliþe gebæro, eac þon breostceare,
sinsorgna gedreag, sy æt him sylfum gelong   45
eal his worulde wyn, sy ful wide fah
feorres folclondes, þæt min freond siteð
under stanhliþe storme behrimed,
wine werigmod, wætre beflowen
on dreorsele. Dreogeð se min wine   50
micle modceare; he gemon to oft
wynlicran wic. Wa bið þam þe sceal
of langoþe leofes abidan.

A joyless dwelling! Full often my heart pains
When I recall my lord's departure. In this world
Lovers are, who live together, sharing the same bed,
When I all alone walk at dawn   35
Under the oak tree, crossing the earth-cave;
There I must sit the long summer's day;
There I can weep over my life in exile,
Many a hardship, for I can never be
Free from this heart's pain of mine,   40
Nor from all the longing that gripped me in this life."

    The young man must ever be in grief,
His thought drenched in sorrow, while he must keep
A cheerful bearing, despite his breast's pain
And sorrow thronging endlessly. All his worldly joy   45
Will depend on him, though he may be banished far
To live in exile in a distant land; my friend sits
Under a rocky slope, frost-bit in storm,
My weary-hearted friend, drenched with rain,
In his dreary dwelling place. My friend endures   50
Great pain and grief; he often recalls
A dwelling more replenished with joy. Woe be with him
Who must wait for his beloved man with longing.

Deor

Welund him be wurman wræces cunnade,
anhydig eorl earfoþa dreag,
hæfde him to gesiþþe sorge ond longaþ,
wintercealde wræce; wean oft onfond,
siþþan hine Niðhad on nede legde,   5
swoncre seonobende on syllan monn.
Þæs ofereode, þisses swa mæg!

Beadohilde ne wæs hyre broþra deaþ
on sefan swa sar swa hyre sylfre þing,
þæt heo gearolice ongieten hæfde   10
þæt heo eacen wæs; æfre ne meahte
þriste geþencan, hu ymb þæt sceolde.
Þæs ofereode, þisses swa mæg!

We þæt Mæðhilde monge gefrugnon
wurdon grundlease Geates frige,   15
þæt hi seo sorglufu slæp ealle binom.
Þæs ofereode, þisses swa mæg!

Ðeodric ahte þritig wintra
Mæringa burg; þæt wæs monegum cuþ.
Þæs ofereode, þisses swa mæg!   20

We geascodan Eormanrices
wylfenne geþoht; ahte wide folc
Gotena rices. Þæt wæs grim cyning.
Sæt secg monig sorgum gebunden,
wean on wenan, wyscte geneahhe   25
þæt þæs cynerices ofercumen wære.
Þæs ofereode, þisses swa mæg!

Weland has gone through affliction by hindrances;
A strong-hearted earl, he has undergone tribulations,
Has had for companionship sorrow and longing,
Winter-cold misery, and often come to learn of woe,
Since Nithhad laid him in fetters by making him,   5
A superior man, limp by cutting his sinews.
    That is all in the past now; so may this be.

For Beaduhild the death of her brother was not
So painful as her own plight in her heart,
When she had readily realized   10
That she was pregnant; she could never
Definitely guess what might be toward about it.
    That is all in the past now; so may this be.

We have heard that the laments of Mæthhild,
The Geatish maiden, turned out groundless,   15
That the sorrowful love deprived her of all sleep;
    That is all in the past now; so may this be.

Theodric dominated for thirty winters
The town of the Mæring people, a fact known to many.
    That is all in the past now; so may this be.   20

We have learned of Eormanric's
Wolfish thought; he widely ruled the folk
Of the realm of the Goths; that was a grueling king.
Many a man sat held captive by sorrow,
Expecting woe, much too often wished   25
That it had been over with the kingdom.
    That is all in the past now; so may this be.

Siteð sorgcearig, sælum bidæled,
on sefan sweorceð, sylfum þinceð
þæt sy endeleas earfoða dæl.   30
Mæg þonne geþencan, þæt geond þas woruld
witig dryhten wendeþ geneahhe,
eorle monegum are gesceawað,
wislicne blæd, sumum weana dæl.
Þæt ic bi me sylfum secgan wille,   35
þæt ic hwile wæs Heodeninga scop,
dryhtne dyre. Me wæs Deor noma.
Ahte ic fela wintra folgað tilne,
holdne hlaford, oþþæt Heorrenda nu,
leoðcræftig monn londryht geþah,   40
þæt me eorla hleo ær gesealde.
    Þæs ofereode, þisses swa mæg!

He sits sorrowful, deprived of joy,
Becomes gloomy in heart; it seems to him
That his share of tribulations is endless;   30
He can then reflect that throughout this world
God in his wisdom frequently goes about,
Shows his mercy to many a man, granting
Unfailing favor, and a share of woe to some.
So I will say about myself,   35
That I for some time was a minstrel of Heden's people,
Dear to my lord; Deor was my name.
I had enjoyed good service for many winters
For my gracious lord, till Heorrenda now,
A man skillful in song-making, received the land-right   40
That the lord of the earls had given to me earlier.
    That is all in the past now; so may this be.

The Battle of Brunanburh

Her Æþelstan cyning, eorla drihten,
beorna beahgifa, and his broðor eac,
Eadmund æþeling, ealdorlangne tir
geslogon æt sæcce sweorda ecgum
ymbe Brunanburh. Bordweal clufan,   5
heowan heaþolinde hamora lafan,
afaran Eadweardes, swa him geæþele wæs
from cneomægum, þæt hi æt campe oft
wiþ laþra gehwæne land ealgodon,
hord and hamas. Hettend crungun,   10
Sceotta leoda and scipflotan
fæge feollan, feld dænnede
secga swate, siðþan sunne up
on morgentid, mære tungol,
glad ofer grundas, godes condel beorht,   15
eces drihtnes, oð sio æþele gesceaft
sah to setle. Þær læg secg mænig
garum ageted, guma norþerna
ofer scild scoten, swilce Scittisc eac,
werig, wiges sæd. Wesseaxe forð   20
ondlongne dæg eorodcistum
on last legdun laþum þeodum,
heowan herefleman hindan þearle
mecum mylenscearpan. Myrce ne wyrndon
heardes hondplegan hæleþa nanum   25
þæra þe mid Anlafe ofer æra gebland
on lides bosme land gesohtun,
fæge to gefeohte. Fife lægun
on þam campstede cyningas giunge,
sweordum aswefede, swilce seofene eac   30
eorlas Anlafes, unrim heriges,

This year King Æthelstan, lord of the earls,
Ring-giver of the warriors, and also his brother,
Prince Eadmund, won in battle
Life-long glory by the blades of swords
At Brunanburh. The sons of Eadweard   5
Cleft the shield-wall, hacked the battle-linden
With the hammers' leavings, as befits the descent
From the ancestors that they often in battle
Against every enemy defended land,
Hoard of treasure and homes. Enemies perished,   10
Scottish people and the ship-borne invaders,
Fell fated to die. The field turned wet
With men's blood since the sun, up
In the morning tide, the glorious star,
Glided over the ground, the bright candle of God,   15
Of the Eternal Lord, till the noble creature
Sank to its seat. There lay many a man,
Pierced with spears; northern man,
Shot over the shield, and also the Scots,
Weary and sated with war. The West-Saxons   20
Chased forth the hated people all day long
With their choicest horse-borne troop, and hacked
Brutally the sea-borne bandits from behind
With sharp swords direct from the smiths.
The Mercians did not decline to have fierce fight   25
With hands to any of those, who sought the land
In the bosom of a ship with Anlaf,
Doomed to die in battle. Young kings,
Five of them, lay on the battlefield,
Put to sleep by swords, and also seven   30
Earls of Anlaf, as well as a countless number of men—

flotan and Sceotta. Þær geflemed wearð
Norðmanna bregu, nede gebeded,
to lides stefne litle weorode;
cread cnear on flot, cyning ut gewat   35
on fealene flod, feorh generede.

Swilce þær eac se froda mid fleame com
on his cyþþe norð, Costontinus,
har hilderinc, hreman ne þorfte
mæca gemanan; he wæs his mæga sceard,   40
freonda gefylled on folcstede,
beslagen æt sæcce, and his sunu forlet
on wælstowe wundun forgrunden,
giungne æt guðe. Gelpan ne þorfte
beorn blandenfeax bilgeslehtes,   45
eald inwidda, ne Anlaf þy ma;
mid heora herelafum hlehhan ne þorftun
þæt heo beaduweorca beteran wurdun
on campstede cumbolgehnastes,
garmittinge, gumena gemotes,   50
wæpengewrixles, þæs hi on wælfelda
wiþ Eadweardes afaran plegodan.
Gewitan him þa Norþmen nægledcnearrum,
dreorig daraða laf, on Dinges mere
ofer deop wæter Difelin secan,   55
eft Iraland, æwiscmode.
Swilce þa gebroþer begen ætsamne,
cyning and æþeling, cyþþe sohton,
Wesseaxena land, wiges hremige.
Letan him behindan hræw bryttian   60
saluwigpadan, þone sweartan hræfn,
hyrnednebban, and þane hasewanpadan,
earn æftan hwit, æses brucan,
grædigne guðhafoc and þæt græge deor,
wulf on wealde. Ne wearð wæl mare   65

Of seamen and the Scots. There the Norsemen's chieftain
Was put to flight, and forced by need,
To the prow of a ship with a small band.
The ship rushed onto the sea; the king departed   35
Out on the dark waves, and saved his life.
Likewise there also the old campaigner fled
North to his folk's region—Constantinus,
The hoary warrior. He had no reason to exult
In the crossing of the swords: he was bereft of kinsmen,   40
Deprived of friends in the battlefield,
Slaughtered in battle; and he left his son
On the battlefield, mangled with wounds,
A fledgling in field-fight. The grizzle-haired man
Had no reason to boast of the sword-slaughter,   45
The old treacherous man, nor Anlaf the more;
With those few survivors left, they had no reason to laugh
That they were the better in the deeds of war,
In the collision of the banners on the battlefield,
In the crossing of the spears, in the clash of men,   50
In the exchange of blows; that on a battlefield
They fought against the sons of Eadweard.
Then the Norsemen departed in the nailed ships,
The sad remnant the spears had spared, to Dinges Mere
Over the deep water to seek Dublin,   55
Ireland again, abashed and crest-fallen.
Likewise the brothers, the two of them together,
King and Prince, sought their folk's region,
The land of the West-Saxons, exulted by victory.
They left the dark-coated creatures behind   60
To feast on the carcasses—the black raven,
Horny-beaked, and the dusky-coated one,
The eagle white in hind, to enjoy the carrion—
The greedy vulture, and that gray animal,
The wolf in the woodland. A greater slaughter   65

on þis eiglande æfre gieta
folces gefylled beforan þissum
sweordes ecgum, þæs þe us secgað bec,
ealde uðwitan, siþþan eastan hider
Engle and Seaxe up becoman,   70
ofer brad brimu Brytene sohtan,
wlance wigsmiþas, Wealas ofercoman,
eorlas arhwate eard begeatan.

Had never occurred yet on this island,
Of people killed before this
By the sword-blades, as the books tell us,
Old learned men, since from the east hither
The Angles and the Saxons came up   70
Over the wide seas, sought Britain,
The proud war-makers, overcame the Welshmen,
The glorious earls conquered the land.

brocen wurde.
Het þa hyssa hwæne hors forlætan,
feor afysan, and forð gangan,
hicgan to handum and to hige godum.
Þa þæt Offan mæg ærest onfunde,   5
þæt se eorl nolde yrhðo geþolian,
he let him þa of handon leofne fleogan
hafoc wið þæs holtes, and to þære hilde stop;
be þam man mihte oncnawan þæt se cniht nolde
wacian æt þam wige, þa he to wæpnum feng.   10
Eac him wolde Eadric his ealdre gelæstan,
frean to gefeohte, ongan þa forð beran
gar to guþe. He hæfde god geþanc
þa hwile þe he mid handum healdan mihte
bord and bradswurd; beot he gelæste   15
þa he ætforan his frean feohtan sceolde.
    Ða þær Byrhtnoð ongan beornas trymian,
rad and rædde, rincum tæhte
hu hi sceoldon standan and þone stede healdan,
and bæd þæt hyra randas rihte heoldon   20
fæste mid folman, and ne forhtedon na.
Þa he hæfde þæt folc fægere getrymmed,
he lihte þa mid leodon þær him leofost wæs,
þær he his heorðwerod holdost wiste.
Þa stod on stæðe, stiðlice clypode   25
wicinga ar, wordum mælde,
se on beot abead brimliþendra
ærænde to þam eorle, þær he on ofre stod:
"Me sendon to þe sæmen snelle,
heton ðe secgan þæt þu most sendan raðe   30
beagas wið gebeorge; and eow betere is

would be broken.
Then he ordered each man to forsake his horse,
Send it far away, and march on foot,
Thinking on what his hands can do and on high spirit.
When Offa's kinsman first realized   5
That the earl would not brook cowardice,
He then let his beloved hawk fly from his hand
To the woods, and stepped onward to the battle-front.
By this one might perceive that the youth would not
Weaken in the battle when he held weapons in his grip.   10
Eadric also wished to serve his prince,
His lord in the battle, for he had borne forth
His spear to a battle-front. He had good cheer
So long as he in his hands could hold
A shield and wield a broad sword. He fulfilled his vow,   15
When in the presence of his lord he had to fight.
      Then Birhtnoth began to array his men there,
Rode around and gave counsels, taught the men
How they should stand and hold the stead,
And bade that they should hold their shields aright,   20
Firmly with their hands, and should not fear.
When he had arrayed the people properly,
He then alighted, where it was most agreeable, to be with those,
Where he knew were his retainers most loyal to him.
Then stood on the bank, loudly cried out   25
The herald of the Vikings, spoke resonantly—
He threateningly delivered the message of his seafaring
Pack to the earl, with his feet firmly set on the bank:
"Bold seamen have sent me to you,
Have asked me to tell you that you may quickly send   30
Treasures for peace's sake; and it is better for you

43

þæt ge þisne garræs mid gafole forgyldon,
þon we swa hearde hilde dælon.
Ne þurfe we us spillan, gif ge spedaþ to þam;
we willað wið þam golde grið fæstnian.   35
Gyf þu þat gerædest, þe her ricost eart,
þæt þu þine leoda lysan wille,
syllan sæmannum on hyra sylfra dom
feoh wið freode, and niman frið æt us,
we willaþ mid þam sceattum us to scype gangan,   40
on flot feran, and eow friþes healdan."
Byrhtnoð maþelode, bord hafenode,
wand wacne æsc, wordum mælde,
yrre and anræd ageaf him andsware:
"Gehyrst þu, sælida, hwæt þis folc segeð?   45
Hi willað eow to gafole garas syllan,
ættrynne ord and ealde swurd,
þa heregeatu þe eow æt hilde ne deah.
Brimmanna boda, abeod eft ongean,
sege þinum leodum miccle laþre spell,   50
þæt her stynt unforcuð eorl mid his werode,
þe wile gealgean eþel þysne,
Æþelredes eard, ealdres mines,
folc and foldan. Feallan sceolon
hæþene æt hilde. To heanlic me þinceð   55
þæt ge mid urum sceattum to scype gangon
unbefohtene, nu ge þus feor hider
on urne eard in becomon.
Ne sceole ge swa softe sinc gegangan;
us sceal ord and ecg ær geseman,   60
grim guðplega, ær we gofol syllon."
Het þa bord beran, beornas gangan,
þæt hi on þam easteðe ealle stodon.
Ne mihte þær for wætere werod to þam oðrum;
þær com flowende flod æfter ebban,   65

That you buy off this spear-raising with tribute,
Than we deal with each other with a bitter battle.
No need for us to destroy each other, if you are rich enough.
We will consolidate truce on the pledge of gold.   35
If you that are the most powerful advise that—
That you will safeguard your people,
Give to the seamen on their own terms
Money for truce, and obtain peace from us,
We will return to our ship with the tribute,   40
Set out on the sea, and keep peace with you."
      Birhtnoth spoke, lifted his shield high,
Waved his slim ash-spear, uttered in words,
Wrathful and resolute, gave him the answer:
"Do you hear, seafaring man, what this folk say?   45
They wish to give spears rather than tribute,
Deadly thrust and old sword,
War-gear, whose use ends with death at a battle.
Messenger of the sea-bandits, take back this answer,
Deliver to your people a message far more hostile—   50
That here stands a nobleman of unblemished fame with his troop,
Who will defend this homeland of ours,
The territory of Æthelred, my prince—
Its people and their homestead land. Heathens are bound
To fall at all battles. It appears to me too much of an ignominy   55
That you should return to your ship with our tribute,
Unopposed, now you have thus far hither
Come deep in our homestead territory.
Nor shall you so easily obtain treasure;
Spear and sword must settle us before,   60
The grim game of war, rather than we offer tribute."
      He then ordered the men to bear shields and march on,
That they all stood on the riverbank.
The water between the troops kept one from the other;
There came the tide flowing in after the ebb,   65

45

lucon lagustreamas. To lang hit him þuhte,
hwænne hi togædere garas beron.
Hi þær Pantan stream mid prasse bestodon,
Eastseaxena ord and se æschere.
Ne mihte hyra ænig oþrum derian,   70
buton hwa þurh flanes flyht fyl gename.
Se flod ut gewat; þa flotan stodon gearowe,
wicinga fela, wiges georne.
Het þa hæleða hleo healdan þa bricge
wigan wigheardne, se wæs haten Wulfstan,   75
cafne mid his cynne, þæt wæs Ceolan sunu,
þe ðone forman man mid his francan ofsceat
þe þær baldlicost on þa bricge stop.
Þær stodon mid Wulfstane wigan unforhte,
Ælf[h]ere and Maccus, modige twegen,   80
þa noldon æt þam forda fleam gewyrcan,
ac hi fæstlice wið ða fynd weredon,
þa hwile þe hi wæpna wealdan moston.
Þa hi þæt ongeaton and georne gesawon
þæt hi þær bricgweardas bitere fundon,   85
ongunnon lytegian þa laðe gystas,
bædon þæt hi upgang agan moston,
ofer þone ford faran, feþan lædan.
    Ða se eorl ongan for his ofermode
alyfan landes to fela laþere ðeode.   90
Ongan ceallian þa ofer cald wæter
Byrht[h]elmes bearn (beornas gehlyston):
"Nu eow is gerymed, gað ricene to us,
guman to guþe; god ana wat
hwa þære wælstowe wealdan mote."   95
Wodon þa wælwulfas (for wætere ne murnon),
wicinga werod, west ofer Pantan,
ofer scir wæter scyldas wegon,
lidmen to lande linde bæron.

The river currents closed in. Too long it seemed to them
Till the time when they could let their spears meet together.
There they stood along the stream of Pant in solemn array—
The East-Saxons' vanguard and the ship-borne troop.
Nor could any of them harm another,   70
Except when one embraces death through an arrow's flight.
The tide receded out; the seamen stood all ready—
Numerous Vikings, ready to run into battle.
Then the warriors' protector ordered a battle-brave one
To keep guard on the bridge—whose name was Wulfstan,   75
A man brave after his lineage. That was Ceola's son,
Who slew with his flying spear whoever is the first
That dared to step most boldly on the bridge.
There stood with Wulfstan fearless fighters,
Ælf[h]ere and Maccus, two brave ones,   80
Who would not take flight from the ford,
But they firmly defended against the enemy,
So long as they could wield weapons.
When they perceived and clearly saw
That they found fierce bridge-guards there,   85
The hateful visitors began to use guile then—
Asked that they might be allowed access to landing,
Go over the ford, and lead the foot-soldiers.
 Then the earl, for his overconfidence, began
To allow the loathsome people to take land a bit too much.   90
Birhthelm's son then began to call out
Over the cold water—which the warriors listened:
"Now for you is the way open, come quickly to us,
Men-at-arms! God alone knows
Who will wield power in the battle-field."   95
The slayer-wolves advanced then—didn't mind the water—
The band of Vikings, westward over Pant,
Over the gleaming water carried their shields,
The sailors bore their linden-wood shields to land.

Þær ongean gramum gearowe stodon   100
Byrhtnoð mid beornum; he mid bordum het
wyrcan þone wihagan, and þæt werod healdan
fæste wið feondum. Þa wæs feohte neh,
tir æt getohte. Wæs seo tid cumen
þæt þær fæge men feallan sceoldon.   105
Þær wearð hream ahafen, hremmas wundon,
earn æses georn; wæs on eorþan cyrm.
Hi leton þa of folman feolhearde speru,
gegrundene garas fleogan;
bogan wæron bysige, bord ord onfeng.   110
   Biter wæs se beaduræs, beornas feollon
on gehwæðere hand, hyssas lagon.
Wund wearð Wulfmær, wælræste geceas,
Byrhtnoðes mæg; he mid billum wearð,
his swuster sunu, swiðe forheawen.   115
Þær wearð wicingum wiþerlean agyfen.
Gehyrde ic þæt Eadweard anne sloge
swiðe mid his swurde, swenges ne wyrnde,
þæt him æt fotum feoll fæge cempa;
þæs him his ðeoden þanc gesæde,   120
þam burþene, þa he byre hæfde.
Swa stemnetton stiðhicgende
hysas æt hilde, hogodon georne
hwa þær mid orde ærost mihte
on fægean men feorh gewinnan,   125
wigan mid wæpnum; wæl feol on eorðan.
Stodon stædefæste; stihte hi Byrhtnoð,
bæd þæt hyssa gehwylc hogode to wige
þe on Denon wolde dom gefeohtan.
Wod þa wiges heard, wæpen up ahof,   130
bord to gebeorge, and wið þæs beornes stop.
Eode swa anræd eorl to þam ceorle,
ægþer hyra oðrum yfeles hogode.

There, ready to meet their ferocious foes, stood 100
Birhtnoth with his men. He ordered with the shields
To form a wall of battle, and that the troop should hold
Fast against the foes. The battle was imminent then,
The glory it would bring, too. The time had come
When the men doomed to die had to fall. 105
There a shouting rose; ravens circled in the air,
The eagle was eager for carrion. On earth was uproar.
They then let from their hands
File-hard spears, the grim-sharpened sticks, fly.
The bows were busy, the shield received sharp thrust. 110
     Fierce was the battle-storm; men fell,
On both sides, youths lay dead.
Wulfmær became wounded, chose death-bed in battle:
A kinsman of Birhtnoth, his sister's son,
He was utterly hewn down by swords. 115
There to the Vikings requital was made.
I have heard that Eadweard struck one
Fiercely with his sword, not relenting the stroke,
That the man doomed to die fell at his feet.
For this his lord gave thanks to him, 120
To his chamberlain, when he had a chance.
Thus men in battle stood firm, unshaken
In their resolution; the men wielding the weapons
Were eager to guess who there might be the first
To take life from any man already fated to fall. 125
Carnage and slaughter fell to cover the earth.
They stood steadfast; Birhtnoth exhorted them,
Bade that each youth who wished to bring doom
To the Danes should give thought only to battle.
Then a war-beaten one trudged on, heaved up his weapon, 130
His shield for protection, and stepped toward the warrior.
No less determined than the low-born man, the earl stepped forward;
Each of them was intent on harming the other.

Sende ða se særinc suþerne gar,
þæt gewundod wearð wigena hlaford; 135
he sceaf þa mid ðam scylde, þæt se sceaft tobærst,
and þæt spere sprengde, þæt hit sprang ongean.
Gegremod wearð se guðrinc; he mid gare stang
wlancne wicing, þe him þa wunde forgeaf.
Frod wæs se fyrdrinc; he let his francan wadan 140
þurh ðæs hysses hals, hand wisode
þæt he on þam færsceaðan feorh geræhte.
Ða he oþerne ofstlice sceat,
þæt seo byrne tobærst; he wæs on breostum wund
þurh ða hringlocan, him æt heortan stod 145
ætterne ord. Se eorl wæs þe bliþra,
hloh þa, modi man, sæde metode þanc
ðæs dægweorces þe him drihten forgeaf.
    Forlet þa drenga sum daroð of handa,
fleogan of folman, þæt se to forð gewat 150
þurh ðone æþelan Æþelredes þegen.
Him be healfe stod hyse unweaxen,
cniht on gecampe, se full caflice
bræd of þam beorne blodigne gar,
Wulfstanes bearn, Wulfmær se geonga, 155
forlet forheardne faran eft ongean;
ord in gewod, þæt se on eorþan læg
þe his þeoden ær þearle geræhte.
Eode þa gesyrwed secg to þam eorle;
he wolde þæs beornes beagas gefecgan, 160
reaf and hringas and gerenod swurd.
Þa Byrhtnoð bræd bill of sceðe,
brad and bruneccg, and on þa byrnan sloh.
To raþe hine gelette lidmanna sum,
þa he þæs eorles earm amyrde. 165
Feoll þa to foldan fealohilte swurd;
ne mihte he gehealdan heardne mece,

Then the sea-faring fighter threw a southern spear,
That might have wounded the lord of the warriors.   135
He shoved with the shield, that the shaft was shattered,
And the spear broken, that it sprang away.
The war-lord became enraged; he pierced with his spear
The proud Viking, who had given him wound.
Experienced was the battle-lord; he let his spear run   140
Through the man's neck, maneuvered his hand
In such a way that he could touch the marauder's life.
Then he quickly pierced another,
That the corselet burst; he was wounded in breast
Through the ring-mail shirt; upon his breast was made   145
A deadly thrust. The earl was in better cheer,
Laughed then the brave man, thanked God
For the day's work that God had given him.
　　　Then a Viking let go from his grip a spear,
Fly from his hand, so that it launched forth,   150
Piercing through Æthelred's noble thane.
Beside him stood a youth not fully grown yet,
Not even ripe for battle; bravely he—
Son of Wulfstan, Wulfmær the young—
Pulled the blood-trickling spear from the war-lord,   155
And flung the hard-beaten spear to fly back again;
The spear-head dug in, that on the earth lay the man,
Who had severely wounded his lord earlier.
Then a man in full arms headed to the earl;
He intended to take precious things from the man—   160
Warlike coat and ringed jacket, as well as the ornamented sword.
Then Birhtnoth drew his sword from the sheath,
Broad and with bright blade, and struck on the mail-coat.
Very quickly one Viking blocked his way,
And inflicted wound on an arm of the earl.   165
Then to the earth fell the sword with a golden hilt;
He could not hold his dreaded sword,

wæpnes wealdan. Þa gyt þæt word gecwæð
har hilderinc, hyssas bylde,
bæd gangan forð gode geferan;   170
ne mihte þa on fotum leng fæste gestandan.
He to heofenum wlat:
"Geþancie þe, ðeoda waldend,
ealra þæra wynna þe ic on worulde gebad.
Nu ic ah, milde metod, mæste þearfe   175
þæt þu minum gaste godes geunne,
þæt min sawul to ðe siðian mote
on þin geweald, þeoden engla,
mid friþe ferian. Ic eom frymdi to þe
þæt hi helsceaðan hynan ne moton."   180
Ða hine heowon hæðene scealcas
and begen þa beornas þe him big stodon,
Ælfnoð and Wul[f]mær begen lagon,
ða onemn hyra frean feorh gesealdon.
Hi bugon þa fram beaduwe þe þær beon noldon.   185
Þær wearð Oddan bearn ærest on fleame,
Godric fram guþe, and þone godan forlet
þe him mænigne oft mear gesealde;
he gehleop þone eoh þe ahte his hlaford,
on þam gerædum þe hit riht ne wæs,   190
and his broðru mid him begen ærndon,
God[w]ine and Godwig, guþe ne gymdon,
ac wendon fram þam wige and þone wudu sohton,
flugon on þæt fæsten and hyra feore burgon,
and manna ma þonne hit ænig mæð wære,   195
gyf hi þa geearnunga ealle gemundon
þe he him to duguþe gedon hæfde.
Swa him Offa on dæg ær asæde
on þam meþelstede, þa he gemot hæfde,
þæt þær modiglice manega spræcon   200
þe eft æt þearfe þolian noldon.

52

Wield his weapon. Nevertheless the word he spoke,
The hoary warrior, instilled courage in the youths,
Bade them to push on bravely together;   170
He could not stand firm on his feet any further.
He turned his eyes to Heaven:
"I thank you, Ruler of peoples,
For all the joys that I have had in this world.
Now, merciful Lord, I have most need   175
That you grant grace upon my spirit,
That my soul may make journey to you,
Upon your power, Prince of angels,
Go in peace. I beseech you
That those demons in Hell do not injure it."   180
      Then the heathen warriors slew him
And both of the men who stood close to him;
Ælfnoth and Wulfmar both lay dead,
When alongside their lord they gave up their lives.
Then those who didn't wish to stay retreated from the battle.   185
There Odda's son, Godric, came to be the first
To flee from the battle; and he deserted the kind man,
Who had often given him many a good horse.
He leaped upon the horse that his lord had owned,
Upon the harness that it was not right for him to hold;   190
And both of his brothers, Godwin and Godwig,
With him galloped away: they cared not about the battle,
But went from the war and sought refuge in the wood,
Fled to that fortress and saved their lives—
And more men than it would be appropriate in any way,   195
If they had remembered all the kind deeds
That he had done for them for their own sake.
So had said to him Offa earlier that day
At an assembly, when he held a meeting,
That many there were speaking big-heartedly,   200
Who would not endure later on at times of need.

Þa wearð afeallen þæs folces ealdor,

Æþelredes eorl; ealle gesawon

heorðgeneatas þæt hyra heorra læg.

Þa ðær wendon forð wlance þegenas,   205

unearge men efston georne;

hi woldon þa ealle oðer twega,

lif forlætan oððe leofne gewrecan.

Swa hi bylde forð bearn Ælfrices,

wiga wintrum geong, wordum mælde,   210

Ælfwine þa cwæð, he on ellen spræc:

"Gemunan þa mæla þe we oft æt meodo spræcon,

þonne we on bence beot ahofon,

hæleð on healle, ymbe heard gewinn;

nu mæg cunnian hwa cene sy.   215

Ic wylle mine æþelo eallum gecyþan,

þæt ic wæs on Myrcon miccles cynnes;

wæs min ealda fæder Ealhelm haten,

wis ealdorman, woruldgesælig.

Ne sceolon me on þære þeode þegenas ætwitan   220

þæt ic of ðisse fyrde feran wille,

eard gesecan, nu min ealdor ligeð

forheawen æt hilde. Me is þæt hearma mæst;

he wæs ægðer min mæg and min hlaford."

Þa he forð eode, fæhðe gemunde,   225

þæt he mid orde anne geræhte

flotan on þam folce, þæt se on foldan læg

forwegen mid his wæpne. Ongan þa winas manian,

frynd and geferan, þæt hi forð eodon.

Offa gemælde, æscholt asceoc: 230

"Hwæt þu, Ælfwine, hafast ealle gemanode

þegenas to þearfe, nu ure þeoden lið,

eorl on eorðan. Us is eallum þearf

þæt ure æghwylc oþerne bylde

wigan to wige, þa hwile þe he wæpen mæge   235

54

Thus came to fall the leader of the people,
Æthelred's earl; all of them saw,
His hearth-friends, that their chieftain had lain slain.
Then there marched forth the proud thanes,   205
Fearless men hastened eagerly forward.
They all wished then one or the other—
Give up life or avenge their beloved man.
Thus Ælfric's son boosted them forth—
A warrior young in winters, he spoke in words—   210
Ælfwine spoke then, uttered thus onto courage:
"I remember the occasion when we often spoke over mead,
When we'd heave our vow aloft on our bench,
Warriors in the hall, to boast of fierce fighting.
Now is the time to find out who is brave.   215
I will make my noble birth known to all—
That I descend in Mercia from a great line of forebears.
My grandfather was Ealhelm, so they called him,
A wise nobleman, blessed with worldly prosperity.
Thanes in that nation must not reproach me   220
That I will depart from this troop of army,
Seek my homeland, now my lord lies,
Slain in battle. That is the greatest sorrow for me;
He was both my kinsman and my lord."
    Then he stepped forth, full of hostile anger,   225
That he with his spear wounded one seaman
In that band, that he fell to the earth, slain
By the weapon he threw. Then he exhorted his friends,
His companions and comrades, that they march on.
Offa spoke, shook his ash-spear: 230
"Yes, Ælfwine, you have well exhorted us all—
Thanes in need. Now our lord, the earl,
Lies on the earth, it is needed for us all
That each one of us boosts up another
Warrior to battle, so long as he may keep   235

habban and healdan, heardne mece,
gar and godswurd. Us Godric hæfð,
earh Oddan bearn, ealle beswicene.

Wende þæs formoni man, þa he on meare rad,
on wlancan þam wicge, þæt wære hit ure hlaford;   240
forþan wearð her on felda folc totwæmed,
scyldburh tobrocen. Abreoðe his angin,
þæt he her swa manigne man aflymde!"

Leofsunu gemælde and his linde ahof,
bord to gebeorge; he þam beorne oncwæð: 245
"Ic þæt gehate, þæt ic heonon nelle
fleon fotes trym, ac wille furðor gan,
wrecan on gewinne minne winedrihten.
Ne þurfon me embe Sturmere stedefæste hælæð
wordum ætwitan, nu min wine gecranc,   250
þæt ic hlafordleas ham siðie,
wende fram wige, ac me sceal wæpen niman,
ord and iren." He ful yrre wod,
feaht fæstlice, fleam he forhogode.

Dunnere þa cwæð, daroð acwehte,   255
unorne ceorl, ofer eall clypode,
bæd þæt beorna gehwylc Byrhtnoð wræce:
"Ne mæg na wandian se þe wrecan þenceð
frean on folce, ne for feore murnan."
Þa hi forð eodon, feores hi ne rohton;   260
ongunnon þa hiredmen heardlice feohtan,
grame garberend, and god bædon
þæt hi moston gewrecan hyra winedrihten
and on hyra feondum fyl gewyrcan.

Him se gysel ongan geornlice fylstan;   265
he wæs on Norðhymbron heardes cynnes,
Ecglafes bearn, him wæs Æscferð nama.
He ne wandode na æt þam wigplegan,
ac he fysde forð flan genehe;

And wield a weapon, whether it be a hard mace,
A spear, or a good sword. Godric, the cowardly
Son of Odda, has deceived us all.
Many thought, when he rode off on that horse,
On that proud steed, that it was our lord.   240
Therefore, here in the field, people were scattered,
The phalanx became shattered. Spit on what he did,
That here he put to flight so many a man!"
 Leofsunu spoke, and heaved his linden-wood,
A shield he needed for self-defense. He answered the man: 245
"I have promised that I will not from here
Flee even one footstep but will step forward,
Avenge in battle my beloved lord.
Steadfast men around Sturmere need not reproach
Me in words, now my lord has demised,   250
If I, a lord-less man, travel home,
Leave the battle behind. But weapon shall take me,
Whether spear or sword." He in full wrath stepped forward,
Fought undauntedly, scorning to flee.
Then Dunnere spoke, brandishing his spear,   255
A man of humble birth, cried out over all,
Bade that each man should avenge Birhtnoth:
"He who wishes to avenge the lord of his folk
Cannot flinch or care about life."
Then they pushed forward, not caring about their lives.   260
The retainers then began to fight hardily,
Ferocious spear-bearing men, and they prayed God
That they be allowed to avenge their dear lord
And upon their enemies inflict destruction.
The hostage began to help them in earnest.   265
He was of brave kin from Northumbria,
Eclaf's son, whose name was Æscferth.
He did not flinch at the game of war;
But he busily shot arrows from his bow.

hwilon he on bord sceat, hwilon beorn tæsde, 270
æfre embe stunde he sealde sume wunde,
þa hwile ðe he wæpna wealdan moste.

Þa gyt on orde stod Eadweard se langa,
gearo and geornful, gylpwordum spræc
þæt he nolde fleogan fotmæl landes, 275
ofer bæc bugan, þa his betera leg.

He bræc þone bordweall and wið þa beornas feaht,
oðþæt he his sincgyfan on þam sæmannum
wurðlice wrec, ær he on wæle læge.

Swa dyde Æþe[l]ric, æþele gefera, 280
fus and forðgeorn, feaht eornoste.

Sibyrhtes broðor and swiðe mænig oþer
clufon cellod bord, cene hi weredon;
bærst bordes lærig, and seo byrne sang
gryreleoða sum. Þa æt guðe sloh 285
Offa þone sælidan, þæt he on eorðan feoll,
and ðær Gaddes mæg grund gesohte.

Raðe wearð æt hilde. Offa forheawen;
he hæfde ðeah geforþod þæt he his frean gehet,
swa he beotode ær wið his beahgifan 290
þæt hi sceoldon begen on burh ridan,
hale to hame, oððe on here crincgan,
on wælstowe wundum sweltan;
he læg ðegenlice ðeodne gehende.

Ða wearð borda gebræc. Brimmen wodon, 295
guðe gegremode; gar oft þurhwod
fæges feorhhus. Forð þa eode Wistan,
Þurstanes sunu, wið þas secgas feaht;
he wæs on geþrange hyra þreora bana,
ær him Wigelines bearn on þam wæle læge. 300
Þær wæs stið gemot; stodon fæste
wigan on gewinne, wigend cruncon,
wundum werige. Wæl feol on eorþan.

Sometimes he shot on a shield, sometimes pierced a man;   270
Ever and each time he inflicted some wound,
So long as he could wield weapons.
    Still in the vanguard stood Eadweard the Long,
Ready and eager, with boasting words spoke
That he would not flee even one footstep,   275
Nor turn away, when his lord lay dead.
He broke the shield-wall and fought against the invaders,
Till he bravely avenged his treasure-giver
Upon the sea-bandits, before he lay on the battlefield.
So did Æthelric, a noble companion,   280
Ready for death and resolute; Brother of Sibirhit,
He fought with determination, and a whole lot of many others
Cleft the . . . shields; they defended bravely.
The shield-rim did burst, and the mail-coat clanged,
A dreadful music to hear! Then in the battle Offa struck   285
The sea-thief, so that he fell on the earth,
And there Gadd's kinsman sought the ground.
In no time in the scuffle Offa came to be hewn down;
He had, though, fulfilled what he had promised his lord,
As he had vowed before to his ring-giver—   290
That they should ride together into the town,
Sound and safe to home, or perish in the midst of the marauders,
Die of wounds in the slaughter-feasting battlefield.
He lay, most like a thane, close to his prince.
    Then crashing of the shields followed. The battle-enraged   295
Sea-robbers pushed forward; spear often went through
The body of one doomed to die. Then onward stepped Wistan,
Son of Thurstan, and against the men he fought.
He was the slayer of three of those in the throng,
Before he fell to lie on the slaughter-yard, this son of Wighelm.   300
There was a stern encounter: stood fast
The warriors in battle; the war-lords perished,
Weary of their wounds. Carnage fell on the earth.

Oswold and Eadwold ealle hwile,
begen þa gebroþru, beornas trymedon,   305
hyra winemagas wordon bædon
þæt hi þær æt ðearfe þolian sceoldon,
unwaclice wæpna neotan.

Byrhtwold maþelode, bord hafenode
(se wæs eald geneat), æsc acwehte;   310
he ful baldlice beornas lærde:
"Hige sceal þe heardra, heorte þe cenre,
mod sceal þe mare, þe ure mægen lytlað.
Her lið ure ealdor eall forheawen,
god on greote. A mæg gnornian   315
se ðe nu fram þis wigplegan wendan þenceð.
Ic eom frod feores; fram ic ne wille,
ac ic me be healfe minum hlaforde,
be swa leofan men, licgan þence."
Swa hi Æþelgares bearn ealle bylde,   320
Godric to guþe. Oft he gar forlet,
wælspere windan on þa wicingas,
swa he on þam folce fyrmest eode,
heow and hynde, oðþæt he on hilde gecranc.
Næs þæt na se Godric þe ða guðe forbeah   325

         *   *   *

60

Oswold and Eadwold, all the while,
Both brothers, encouraged the men,   305
Bade their beloved kinsmen in words
That they there at need should endure,
Use the weapons without flinching to weakness.
Birhtwold spoke, lifted up his shield,
(He was an old retainer), brandished his ash-spear;   310
He advised the men full boldly:
"Mind must be the harder, heart the keener,
Courage must be the greater, the less grows our might.
Here lies our lord all hewn up,
Good man in the dirt. Ever may mourn   315
He that now from the game of war thinks of turning.
I am old of life; I will not from,
But I side by side with my lord,
By so dear a man, think of lying."
So the son of Æthelgar boosted them all,   320
This Godric did, to battle. Often he let spear go,
The deadly shaft flying onto the Vikings;
So he marched on foremost among the folk,
Hewed and slew till he himself fell at battle.
That was not the Godric who fled the battle   325

    *   *   *

The Battle of Finnsburh

nas byrnað?"

Hnæf hleoþrode ða, heaþogeong cyning:
"Ne ðis ne dagað eastan, ne her draca ne fleogeð,
ne her ðisse healle hornas ne byrnað.
Ac her forþ berað; fugelas singað,   5
gylleð græghama, guðwudu hlynneð,
scyld scefte oncwyð. Nu scyneð þes mona
waðol under wolcnum. Nu arisað weadæda
ðe ðisne folces nið fremman willað.
Ac onwacnigeað nu, wigend mine,   10
habbað eowre linda, hicgeaþ on ellen,
winnað on orde, wesað onmode!"
    Ða aras mænig goldhladen ðegn, gyrde hine his swurde.
Ða to dura eodon drihtlice cempan,
Sigeferð and Eaha, hyra sword getugon,   15
and æt oþrum durum Ordlaf and Guþlaf,
and Hengest sylf hwearf him on laste.
    Ða gyt Garulf Guðere styrde
ðæt he swa freolic feorh forman siþe
to ðære healle durum hyrsta ne bære,   20
nu hyt niþa heard anyman wolde,
ac he frægn ofer eal undearninga,
deormod hæleþ, hwa ða duru heolde.
"Sigeferþ is min nama," cwæþ he, "ic eom Secgena leod,
wreccea wide cuð; fæla ic weana gebad,   25
heardra hilda. Ðe is gyt her witod
swæþer ðu sylf to me secean wylle."
    Ða wæs on healle wælslihta gehlyn;
sceolde cellod bord cenum on handa,
banhelm berstan (buruhðelu dynede),   30
oð æt ðære guðe Garulf gecrang,

Then spoke Hnæf, the king young in battle:
"It will not dawn in the east; neither will a dragon fly here,
Nor will the gables of this hall burn;
But here men will bear arms forth, birds shriek,   5
Gray-coated wolf will howl, battle-wood whistle,
Shield will answer the shaft of spear. Now the moon shines,
Wandering beneath the clouds; now woeful deeds will be done,
That will bring about enmity-laden strife and feud of folk.
Yet be alert now, my warriors,   10
Hold high your shields, keep your thoughts on valor,
Fight at the front line, be of resolve in courage!"
      Then up stood many a gold-bedecked thane, girded with sword;
Then to the door stepped the noble warriors,
Sigeferth and Eaha, drew their swords,   15
And at the other door Ordlaf and Guthlaf,
And Hengest himself followed after.
Then Guthere urged Garulf,
That he not bear arms to the hall door
To risk his precious life at the first charge,   20
Now that a battle-hardy one would take it;
But a bold-hearted man, in bold-clear voice,
He asked, for all to hear, who was guarding the door.
"Sigeferth is my name," said he, "I am of the Secgan stock,
An exile known far and wide; many a woe I've lived through,   25
In brutal battles; whichever you will seek from me,
Either life or death, is already decreed here."
 Then in the hall was the din of slaughters;
Embossed shield held by the brave in hand,
The bone-guarding board did burst; the hall-floor resounded,   30
Till in the scuffle Garulf fell down,

ealra ærest eorðbuendra,
Guðlafes sunu, ymbe hyne godra fæla,
hwearflicra hræw. Hræfen wandrode,
sweart and sealobrun. Swurdleoma stod,   35
swylce eal Finnsburuh fyrenu wære.
Ne gefrægn ic næfre wurþlicor æt wera hilde
sixtig sigebeorna sel gebæran,
ne nefre swetne medo sel forgyldan
ðonne Hnæfe guldan his hægstealdas.   40
Hig fuhton fif dagas, swa hyra nan ne feol
drihtgesiða, ac hig ða duru heoldon.
    Ða gewat him wund hæleð on wæg gangan,
sæde þæt his byrne abrocen wære,
heresceorp unhror, and eac wæs his helm ðyrel.   45
Ða hine sona frægn folces hyrde,
hu ða wigend hyra wunda genæson,
oððe hwæþer ðæra hyssa

  * * *

First of all earth-dwellers,
Son of Guthlaf, many good men near him,
The bodies of the brave; black and sallow-brown,
A raven circled above. Sword-beam gleamed,   35
As if the whole Finnsburg were on fire.
Never have I heard of men in battle who fought
More worthily than the sixty honorable warriors,
Nor of young men who repaid better for the shining mead,
Than the young retainers of Hnæf who repaid their lord.   40
They fought five days, yet none of them fell,
His loyal retainers, but they kept the doors.
     Then a wounded warrior departed to go away,
Said that his mail-coat was torn to pieces,
His armor all shattered, and also was his helm pierced.   45
Then the guardian of the people asked him soon,
How the warriors had survived their wounds,
Or whether of those young men
          *   *   *

The Ruin

Wrætlic is þes wealstan, wyrde gebræcon;
burgstede burston, brosnað enta geweorc.
Hrofas sind gehrorene, hreorge torras,
hrungeat berofen, hrim on lime,
scearde scurbeorge scorene, gedrorene,   5
ældo undereotone. Eorðgrap hafað
waldend wyrhtan forweorone, geleorene,
heardgripe hrusan, oþ hund cnea
werþeoda gewitan. Oft þæs wag gebad
ræghar ond readfah rice æfter oþrum,   10
ofstonden under stormum; steap geap gedreas.
[Wunað] giet se [wealstan wederum geheawen],
fel on [. . . .]
grimme gegrunden [. . . . .
. . . .] scan heo[.   15
. . . .]g orþonc ærsceaft [. . . .
. . . .]g[. .] lamrindum beag
mod mo[. . . . . .]yne swiftne gebrægd
hwætred in hringas, hygerof gebond
weallwalan wirum wundrum togædre.   20
Beorht wæron burgræced, burnsele monige,
heah horngestreon, heresweg micel,
meodoheall monig [a rune letter] dreama full,
oþþæt þæt onwende wyrd seo swiþe.
Crungon walo wide, cwoman woldagas,   25
swylt eall fornom secgrofra wera;
wurdon hyra wigsteal westen staþolas,
brosnade burgsteall. Betend crungon
hergas to hrusan. Forþon þas hofu dreorgiað,
ond þæs teaforgeapa tigelum sceadeð   30
hrostbeages hrof. Hryre wong gecrong

Wondrous is this wall-stone; yet Fate has demolished,
Burst the fortress; so the work of the giants crumbles.
Roofs are fallen off, the towers are ruinous,
The frosty gate destroyed, frost settled on lime;
The buildings cracked are torn, collapsing,   5
And crumbling in the flow of time; earth-grip has
The master-builders perished and gone—
The hard grip of the earth has—till a hundred generations
Of people have passed; often this wall has experienced,
Gray with moss, and reddened with rust, kingdom after kingdom, 10
Enduring under storms; high and wide, it has collapsed.
Yet the wall-stone remains, though gashed by weather. . . .
. . . .
. . . .
. . . .   15
. . . .
. . . .
. . . . .   wove together into the rings
A swift ingenuity, and the resolute one bound
The wall-braces with wires wonderfully together;   20
Bright were the fortresses; there were many bathing halls,
A high abundance of gables; great noise of an army,
Many a mead-hall full [of the joys of men,]
Till Fate changed all that utterly;
The slaughtered men fell far and wide; the days of pestilence came, 25
Death took all of the brave men;
Their places of worship became deserted,
And the town decayed. The menders of the buildings died,
The pagan sanctuaries in earth; therefore, the buildings grow desolate,
And the red curved roof parts from the tiles   30
Of the ceiling vault; ruin swept the ground,

gebrocen to beorgum, þær iu beorn monig
glædmod ond goldbeorht, gleoma gefrætwed,
wlonc ond wingal wighyrstum scan;
seah on sinc, on sylfor, on searogimmas,   35
on ead, on æht, on eorcanstan,
on þas beorhtan burg bradan rices.
Stanhofu stodan, stream hate wearp
widan wylme; weal eall befeng
beorhtan bosme, þær þa baþu wæron,   40
hat on hreþre. Þæt wæs hyðelic. . . .

Shattered to mounds of stone, where once many a man,
Joyful and bright with gold, adorned with splendor,
Shone with war trappings, proud and wine-flushed;
They cast their eyes on treasure, on silver, on precious stones,   35
On wealth, on property, on jewelry,
In the bright town of the expansive kingdom;
Stone-buildings stood, hot stream flowed
In a wide surge; all wall surrounded
The bright center, where the baths were,   40
Hot in the heart. That was convenient. . . .

Waldere

I

hyrde hyne georne:

"Huru Welande[.] worc ne geswiceð

monna ænigum ðara ðe Mimming can

heardne gehealdan. Oft æt hilde gedreas

swatfag and sweordwund secg æfter oðrum.   5

Ætlan ordwyga, ne læt ðin ellen nu gy[.]

gedreosan to dæge, dryhtscipe * * *

[. .] is se dæg cumen

þæt ðu scealt aninga oðer twega,

lif forleosan oððe l[. .]gne dom   10

agan mid eldum, Ælfheres sunu.

Nalles ic ðe, wine min, wordum cide,

ðy ic ðe gesawe æt ðam sweordplegan

ðurh edwitscype æniges monnes

wig forbugan oððe on weal fleon,   15

lice beorgan, ðeah þe laðra fela

ðinne byrnhomon billum heowun,

ac ðu symle furðor feohtan sohtest,

mæl ofer mearce; ðy ic ðe metod ondred,

þæt ðu to fyrenlice feohtan sohtest   20

æt ðam ætstealle oðres monnes,

wigrædenne. Weorða ðe selfne

godum dædum, ðenden ðin god recce.

Ne murn ðu for ði mece; ðe wearð maðma cyst

gifeðe to geoce, mid ðy ðu Guðhere scealt   25

beot forbigan, ðæs ðe he ðas beaduwe ongan

[. .]d unryhte ærest secan.

Forsoc he ðam swurde and ðam syncfatum,

beaga mænigo, nu sceal bega leas

I

         . . . . urged him eagerly:
"Certainly the work of Weland will not fail
For any of the men, of those who can grip the hardy
Sword Mimming. Often at battle man after another
Fell, besmeared in blood and wounded by blades.   5
You, fighting man of Attila, let not your valor now yet
Fail you today, your lordly virtue. . . .
         . . . . is the day come
That you must choose one or the other—
Lose your life, or attain [long-lasting] fame   10
Among men— you, son of Ælfhere.
Never shall I chide you, my lord, in words
That I saw you at the sword-blow
Shamefully flinch from the assault
Of any man, or flee onto a wall   15
To save your life, though many enemies
Had your corselet hacked with swords—
But you always sought to fight further,
Well beyond measure; for that I feared for your fate—
That you sought to fight too fiercely   20
In the hostile encounter with another man
At battle. Bring honor to yourself
By brave deeds while God's care guards you.
Do not fear for your sword: the best treasure became yours
By fate's decree for your support; with it you shall   25
Crack the vow of Guthhere, for he first began
To seek this battle unrighteous;
He rejected the sword and the precious cups,
The numerous rings; now he shall, without rings,

hworfan from ðisse hilde, hlafurd secan   30
ealdne [a rune letter] oððe her ær swefan,
gif he ða"   *   *   *

II

"ce bæteran
buton ðam anum ðe ic eac hafa
on stanfate stille gehided.
Ic wat þæt hit ðohte Ðeodric Widian
selfum onsendon, and eac sinc micel   5
maðma mid ði mece, monig oðres mid him
golde gegirwan (iulean genam),
þæs ðe hine of nearwum Niðhades mæg,
Welandes bearn, Widia ut forlet;
ðurh fifela gewe[.]ld forð onette."   10
    Waldere ma[.]ode, wiga ellenrof,
hæfde him on handa hildefrofre,
guðbilla gripe, gyddode wordum:
"Hwæt! Ðu huru wendest, wine Burgenda,
þæt me Hagenan hand hilde gefremede   15
and getwæmde [. .]ðewigges. Feta, gyf ðu dyrre,
æt ðus heaðuwerigan hare byrnan.
Standeð me her on eaxelum Ælfheres laf,
god and geapneb, golde geweorðod,
ealles unscende æðelinges reaf   20
to habbanne, þonne hand wereð
feorhhord feondum. Ne bið fah wið me,
þonne [. .] unmægas eft ongynnað,
mecum gemetað, swa ge me dydon.
Ðeah mæg sige syllan se ðe symle byð   25
recon and rædfest ryh[.]a gehwilces.
Se ðe him to ðam halgan helpe gelifeð,
to gode gioce, he þær gearo findeð

72

Turn back from this battle, a lord seeking his   30
Old homestead, or shall here sleep in death before,
If he. . . ."

II

"". . . a better [sword]
Except the one that I also have
Secretly kept in a stone-embedded sheath.
I know that Theodric thought to send it
To Widia, himself, and also a great hoard   5
Of treasure with the sword, to adorn much
Further with gold. Nithhad's kinsman,
Son of Weland, Widia obtained compensation
For that he had released him from confinement;
Through the realm of the monsters he hurried forth."   10
     Waldere spoke, the brave warrior;
He had in his hand the help in battle,
The battle-bill in his grip, and poured the torrential words:
"Hear me—you, Burgundian breed, surely thought
That Hagen's hand would perform a deed in despite of me,   15
And would thwart me [in the fray]; take, if you dare,
The gray corselet from me, so weary of battle.
Here on my shoulders is borne the heirloom of Ælfhere,
Good and wide-meshed, bedecked with gold,
A glorious armor by all means for a prince   20
To wear when his hand keeps guard of
His soul amongst his foes; it will not betray me
When the hostile ones attempt an assault again,
Encounter me with swords, as you have done to me.
Nevertheless He who is always ready and resolute   25
In each case of [right] can vouchsafe victory;
He who holds trust in the Holy One for help,
In God for rescue—he will find ready there

*   *   *

gif ða earnunga ær geðenceð.

Þonne moten wlance welan britnian,   30
æhtum wealdan, þæt is *   *   *"

*   *   *

If he thinks beforehand on what the merits are.
Then may the Lofty One dispense our weal,   30
Bring about prosperity; that is. . . ."

Widsith

Widsið maðolade, wordhord onleac,
se þe monna mæst mægþa ofer eorþan,
folca geondferde; oft he on flette geþah
mynelicne maþþum. Him from Myrgingum
æþele onwocon. He mid Ealhhilde,   5
fælre freoþuwebban, forman siþe
Hreðcyninges ham gesohte
eastan of Ongle, Eormanrices,
wraþes wærlogan. Ongon þa worn sprecan:
"Fela ic monna gefrægn mægþum wealdan!   10
Sceal þeodna gehwylc þeawum lifgan,
eorl æfter oþrum eðle rædan,
se þe his þeodenstol geþeon wile.
Þara wæs Hwala hwile selast,
ond Alexandreas ealra ricost   15
monna cynnes, ond he mæst geþah
þara þe ic ofer foldan gefrægen hæbbe.
Ætla weold Hunum, Eormanric Gotum,
Becca Baningum, Burgendum Gifica.
Casere weold Creacum ond Cælic Finnum,   20
Hagena Holmrygum ond Heoden Glommum.
Witta weold Swæfum, Wada Hælsingum,
Meaca Myrgingum, Mearchealf Hundingum.
Þeodric weold Froncum, Þyle Rondingum,
Breoca Brondingum, Billing Wernum.   25
Oswine weold Eowum ond Ytum Gefwulf,
Fin Folcwalding Fresna cynne.
Sigehere lengest Sædenum weold,
Hnæf Hocingum, Helm Wulfingum,
Wald Woingum, Wod Þyringum,   30
Sæferð Sycgum, Sweom Ongendþeow,

Widsith spoke, unpacked his hoard of words,
He who of men had traveled most over the earth
Through clans and folks; he had often received in hall
Much envied treasure. From the Myrging tribe
His forebears sprang. With Ealhhild,   5
Fair peace-weaver, in his early voyage,
From the east away from Angle, he sought
The home of Eormanric, king of the Goths,
Blunt breaker of his oaths. He then began to tell many tales:
"Many a man ruling the folks have I heard about.   10
Every prince must live within the bound of custom,
Each earl after another ruling his native land,
One who wishes his princely state to prosper.
Among them was Hwala the best for some time,
And Alexander most powerful of all   15
The race of men, and he thrived most,
Of those I have heard say all over the earth.
Attila ruled the Huns, Eormanric the Goths,
Becca the Banings, Gifica the Burgundians.
Caesar ruled the Greeks, and Caelic the Finns;   20
Hagena ruled the Holmrygs, and Heoden the Glomms.
Witta ruled the Swabians, Wada the Hælsings,
Meaca the Myrgings, Markhalf the Hundings,
Theodric ruled the Franks, Thyle the Rondings,
Breoca the Brondings, and Billing the Wernas.   25
Oswine ruled the Eowas, and Gefwulf the Jutes,
Fin Folcwalding the clan of the Frisians.
Sigehere longest ruled the Sea-Danes,
Hnaef the Hocings, Helm the Wulfings,
Wald the Woings, Wod the Thrings,   30
Sæferth the Sycgians, Ongentheow the Swedes,

Sceafthere Ymbrum, Sceafa Longbeardum,
Hun Hætwerum ond Holen Wrosnum.
Hringweald wæs haten Herefarena cyning.

Offa weold Ongle, Alewih Denum;   35
se wæs þara manna modgast ealra,
no hwæþre he ofer Offan eorlscype fremede,
ac Offa geslog ærest monna,
cnihtwesende, cynerica mæst.
Nænig efeneald him eorlscipe maran   40
on orette. Ane sweorde
merce gemærde wið Myrgingum
bi Fifeldore; heoldon forð siþþan
Engle ond Swæfe, swa hit Offa geslog.
Hroþwulf ond Hroðgar heoldon lengest   45
sibbe ætsomne suhtorfædran,
siþþan hy forwræcon wicinga cynn
ond Ingeldes ord forbigdan,
forheowan æt Heorote Heaðobeardna þrym.
    Swa ic geondferde fela fremdra londa   50
geond ginne grund. Godes ond yfles
þær ic cunnade cnosle bidæled,
freomægum feor folgade wide.
Forþon ic mæg singan ond secgan spell,
mænan fore mengo in meoduhealle   55
hu me cynegode cystum dohten.
Ic wæs mid Hunum ond mid Hreðgotum,
mid Sweom ond mid Geatum ond mid Suþdenum.
Mid Wenlum ic wæs ond mid Wærnum ond mid wicingum.
Mid Gefþum ic wæs ond mid Winedum ond mid Gefflegum.   60
Mid Englum ic wæs ond mid Swæfum ond mid Ænenum.
Mid Seaxum ic wæs ond Sycgum ond mid Sweordwerum.
Mid Hronum ic wæs ond mid Deanum ond mid Heaþo-reamum.
Mid Þyringum ic wæs ond mid Þrowendum,
ond mid Burgendum, þær ic beag geþah;   65

Sceafthere the Ymbians, Sceafa the Longbeards,
Hun ruled the Haetweras, and Holen the Wrosnas.
Hringweald was called king of the predatory bandits.
Offa ruled Angle, Alewih the Danes;   35
He was of all these men the most courageous;
Yet he did not excel over Offa in soldierly spirit,
For Offa, for the first time, of all men, gained
The largest kingdom, in his youthful days;
None of his age proved more fearsome   40
As a warrior; with a single sword
He drew the frontline against the Myrgings,
Fighting near Fifeldor; thenceforth they held,
The Angles and the Swabians, as Offa had gained it.
Hrothwulf and Hrothgar, uncle and nephew,   45
Held ties of kinship together longest,
Since they expelled the band of the Vikings
And suppressed the vanguard of Ingeld, and did
Dispel the throng of the Heathobards at Heorot.
    "So have I traveled many foreign lands   50
Over the grand ground; good and evil
Have I witnessed there; removed from blood-kin,
Away from my kin's blood, I have wandered wide.
So much so that I can sing and tell my story,
Relate before a multitude in the mead-hall   55
How the high-born men graced me with their bounty.
I was with the Huns, and with the Hreth-Goths,
With the Swedes, and with the Geats, and with the South-Danes.
With the Wenlas I was, and with the Wærnas, and with the Vikings.
With the Gefthas I was, and with the Winedas, and with the Gefflegas. 60
With the Angles I was, and with the Swabians, and with the Æneas.
With the Saxons I was, and the Sycgans, and with the Sword-weras.
With the Hronas I was, and with the Danes, and with the Heathoreamas.
With the Thyrings I was, and with the Throwendas,
And with the Burgundians, where I was graced with a jewel;   65

me þær Guðhere forgeaf glædlicne maþþum
songes to leane. Næs þæt sæne cyning!
Mid Froncum ic wæs ond mid Frysum ond mid Frumtingum.
Mid Rugum ic wæs ond mid Glommum ond mid Rumwalum.
Swylce ic wæs on Eatule mid Ælfwine,   70
se hæfde moncynnes, mine gefræge,
leohteste hond lofes to wyrcenne,
heortan unhneaweste hringa gedales,
beorhtra beaga, bearn Eadwines.
Mid Sercingum ic wæs ond mid Seringum;   75
mid Creacum ic wæs ond mid Finnum ond mid Casere,
se þe winburga geweald ahte,
wiolena ond wilna, ond Wala rices.
Mid Scottum ic wæs ond mid Peohtum ond mid Scridefinnum;
mid Lidwicingum ic wæs ond mid Leonum ond mid Longbeardum, 80
mid hæðnum ond mid hæleþum ond mid Hundingum.
Mid Israhelum ic wæs ond mid Exsyringum,
mid Ebreum ond mid Indeum ond mid Egyptum.
Mid Moidum ic wæs ond mid Persum ond mid Myrgingum,
ond Mofdingum ond ongend Myrgingum,   85
ond mid Amothingum. Mid Eastþyringum ic wæs
ond mid Eolum ond mid Istum ond Idumingum.
Ond ic wæs mid Eormanrice ealle þrage,
þær me Gotena cyning gode dohte;
se me beag forgeaf, burgwarena fruma,   90
on þam siex hund wæs smætes goldes,
gescyred sceatta scillingrime;
þone ic Eadgilse on æht sealde,
minum hleodryhtne, þa ic to ham bicwom,
leofum to leane, þæs þe he me lond forgeaf,   95
mines fæder eþel, frea Myrginga.
Ond me þa Ealhhild oþerne forgeaf,
dryhtcwen duguþe, dohtor Eadwines.
Hyre lof lengde geond londa fela,

There Guthhere gave me a glittering treasure
To reward a song—that was not a niggardly king.
  With the Franks I was, and with the Frisians, and with the Frumtings.
With the Rugas I was, and with the Glommas, and with the Romans.
I was also in Italy with Ælfwine;   70
From what I have heard, he had, of all men,
A hand most agile in attaining good fame,
A heart most ready to bestow rings,
Bright jewels—this son of Eadwine did.
With the Saracens I was, and with the Serings.   75
With the Greeks I was, and with the Finns, and with Caesar,
He who possessed the rule of prosperous citadels,
Wealth and the wished-for, and the kingdom of Wales.
  With the Scots I was, and with the Picts, and with the Scride-Finns.
With the Lid-Vikings I was, and with the Leonas, and with the Longbeards,   80
With heathens, and with heroes, and with the Hundings.
With the Israelites I was, and with the Assyrians,
With the Hebrews, and with the Indians, and with the Egyptians.
With the Medes I was, and with the Persians, and with the Myrgings
And the Mofdings and against the Myrgings,   85
And with the Amothingas. With the East-Thyrings I was,
And with the Eolas, and with the Iste and the Idumingas.
And I was with Eormanric; at all times
There the king of the Goths was good to me;
He, lord of the stronghold-occupants, gave me a ring,   90
For which six hundred was to be settled in sceats,
When measured in shilling for pure gold.
I gave it to Eadgils, my lord-protector,
For his keeping, when I returned home,
To repay the dear one for the land he had granted me,   95
My father's estate, what the lord of the Myrgings had done.
And then Ealhhild, her majesty queen,
Daughter of Eadwine, gave me another.
Her fame I spread through many a land,

þonne ic be songe secgan sceolde   100
hwær ic under swegle selast wisse
goldhrodene cwen giefe bryttian.
Ðonne wit Scilling sciran reorde
for uncrum sigedryhtne song ahofan,
hlude bi hearpan hleoþor swinsade,   105
þonne monige men, modum wlonce,
wordum sprecan, þa þe wel cuþan,
þæt hi næfre song sellan ne hyrdon.
    Ðonan ic ealne geondhwearf eþel Gotena,
sohte ic a gesiþa þa selestan;   110
þæt wæs innweorud Earmanrices.
Heðcan sohte ic ond Beadecan ond Herelingas,
Emercan sohte ic ond Fridlan ond Eastgotan,
frodne ond godne fæder Unwenes.
Seccan sohte ic ond Beccan, Seafolan ond Þeodric,   115
Heaþoric ond Sifecan, Hliþe ond Incgenþeow.
Eadwine sohte ic ond Elsan, Ægelmund ond Hungar,
ond þa wloncan gedryht Wiþmyrginga.
Wulfhere sohte ic ond Wyrmhere; ful oft þær wig ne alæg,
þonne Hræda here heardum sweordum   120
ymb Wistlawudu wergan sceoldon
ealdne eþelstol Ætlan leodum.
Rædhere sohte ic ond Rondhere, Rumstan ond Gislhere,
Wiþergield ond Freoþeric, Wudgan ond Haman;
ne wæran þæt gesiþa þa sæmestan,   125
þeah þe ic hy anihst nemnan sceolde.
Ful oft of þam heape hwinende fleag
giellende gar on grome þeode;
wræccan þær weoldan wundnan golde
werum ond wifum, Wudga ond Hama.   130
    Swa ic þæt symle onfond on þære feringe,
þæt se biþ leofast londbuendum
se þe him god syleð gumena rice

Whenever it was my turn to tell in a song   100
Where under the sky I knew the noblest queen,
A gold-bedecked grace, glad to bestow gifts.
When Scilling and I in clear voice,
Before our liege-lord, heaved a song,
Loud to the harp the lay sounded melodious.   105
Then many men who could rightly tell,
Elated in their mood, affirmed in words
That they had never heard a better song.
    Thence I wandered through the entire land of the Goths;
Ever I sought the best of companions—   110
That was the household of Eormanric.
I sought Hethca and Beadeca and the Herelingas;
I sought Emerca and Fridla and Eastgotha,
The old and wise man, father of Unwen.
I sought Secca and Becca, Seafola and Theodric,   115
Heathoric and Sifeca, Hlithe and Incgentheow.
I sought Eadwine and Elsa, Ægelmund and Hungar
And the proud pack of the Withmyrgings.
I sought Wulfhere and Wyrmhere; full often there war continued
When the troop of Hræda with their strong swords,   120
Near the Wistla wood, had to defend their
Ancient territory from the people of Attila.
I sought Rædhere and Rondhere, Rumstan and Gislhere,
Withergield and Freotheric, Wudga and Hama;
They were not my worst associates, though   125
I have had to name them in the last place.
Full often from the band the swishing spear
Flew hissing into the enemy troop;
Men in exile, Wudga and Hama, held sway there
Over men and women with twisted gold.   130
    So I have always found it during my wayfaring,
That he who is the dearest to the dwellers in a land
Is the one to whom God grants rule of men

to gehealdenne, þenden he her leofað."

Swa scriþende gesceapum hweorfað   135
gleomen gumena geond grunda fela,
þearfe secgað, þoncword sprecaþ,
simle suð oþþe norð sumne gemetað
gydda gleawne, geofum unhneawne,
se þe fore duguþe wile dom aræran,   140
eorlscipe æfnan, oþþæt eal scæceð,
leoht ond lif somod; lof se gewyrceð,
hafað under heofonum heahfæstne dom.

To maintain while he lives here."
So the gleemen for men go wandering   135
Through many lands, as fate decrees,
Bespeak what they need, utter words of thanks;
Whether south or north, they always meet someone
Appreciative of songs and bounteous in gift,
One who wishes to extol his glory before his thanes,   140
Fulfill kingly virtues, till all passes away,
Light and life together. He who attains fame
Has under the heavens high-fixed glory.

The Husband's Message

Nu ic onsundran þe secgan wille
[. . . . . . .] treocyn ic tudre aweox;
in mec æld[. . . . .] sceal ellor londes
settan [. . . . .] sealte streamas
[. . . . .]sse. Ful oft ic on bates   5
[. . . . .] gesohte
þær mec mondryhten min [. . . . . .]
ofer heah hofu; eom nu her cumen
on ceolþele, ond nu cunnan scealt
hu þu ymb modlufan mines frean   10
on hyge hycge. Ic gehatan dear
þæt þu þær tirfæste treowe findest.

Hwæt, þec þonne biddan het se þisne beam agrof
þæt þu sinchroden sylf gemunde
on gewitlocan wordbeotunga,   15
þe git on ærdagum oft gespræcon,
þenden git moston on meoduburgum
eard weardigan, an lond bugan,
freondscype fremman. Hine fæhþo adraf
of sigeþeode; heht nu sylfa þe   20
lustum læran, þæt þu lagu drefde,
siþþan þu gehyrde on hliþes oran
galan geomorne geac on bearwe.
Ne læt þu þec siþþan siþes getwæfan,
lade gelettan lifgendne monn.   25

Ongin mere secan, mæwes eþel,
onsite sænacan, þæt þu suð heonan
ofer merelade monnan findest,
þær se þeoden is þin on wenum.
Ne mæg him worulde willa gelimpan   30
mara on gemyndum, þæs þe he me sægde,

. . . .
. . . .
. . . .
. . . .
. . . . Full often in the bosom   5
Of a boat I . . . .   sought,
Where my liege lord . . .   me . . . .
Over the high seas; I have now come here
In a ship, and now you shall know
How concerning the heart's love of my lord   10
You should think in your mind. I dare promise
That you will there find glorious fidelity.

    Look, he, who carved this wood, then ordered me
To implore you, richly adorned, to bring back
The memory of the plights and promises to your mind,   15
That you two agreed upon in olden days,
While you two could in the mead cities
Occupy an abode, inhabit the same estate,
And openly show your mutual love. A feud drove him away
From his powerful kinsfolk. He himself has ordered me now   20
To persuade you that you joyfully should stir the sea,
When you have heard from the hillside's edge
The sad cuckoo-bird sings in the grove.
Then allow not any living man to turn you
Away from the journey, or hinder the course.   25

    Get on your way to seek the sea, the seagull's domain;
Get on board a ship, so that you to the south from here
May find the man when the sea-track is over;
There your prince is waiting for you to arrive.
No greater desire can happen to him in the world   30
In his mind, according to what he said to me,

þonne inc geunne alwaldend god

[. . . . .] ætsomne siþþan motan

secgum ond gesiþum s[. . . . . . .]

n_glede beagas; he genoh hafað   35

fædan gold[.]s [. . . . .]

. . . .]d elþeode eþel healde,

fægre foldan [. . . . .

. . . . .]ra hæleþa, þeah þe her min wine[. . . . .]

nyde gebæded, nacan ut aþrong,   40

ond on yþa geong [. . . . . .] sceolde

faran on flotweg, forðsiþes georn,

mengan merestreamas. Nu se mon hafað

wean oferwunnen; nis him wilna gad,

ne meara ne maðma ne meododreama,   45

ænges ofer eorþan eorlgestreona,

þeodnes dohtor, gif he þin beneah.

Ofer eald gebeot incer twega,

gehyre ic ætsomne [two rune letters] geador

[two rune letters] ond [one rune letter] aþe benemnan,   50

þæt he þa wære ond þa winetreowe

be him lifgendum læstan wolde,

þe git on ærdagum oft gespræconn.

Than that the almighty God may grant you two
To be together and afterwards be able to
Distribute treasure, the studded bracelets,
To men and companions. He has enough   35
Of burnished gold, ...
Throughout the foreign people he holds domain,
Fair earth . . . .
Of devoted men, though here my friend. . . .
Compelled by necessity, pushed out a boat,   40
And on the expanses of waves alone had to
Voyage on the sea, and eager for departure,
Stir up the sea-currents. Now the man has
Overcome his woes; he does not lack desired things—
Horses, treasures, pleasures in the mead-hall,   45
Any of the noble treasures on earth,
A prince's daughter—if he owns you.
Concerning the old promise of you two,
I hear together S and R sounding at the same time,
EA, W, and M to declare by oath   50
That he would fulfill while being alive
The pledge and plight of lifelong fidelity,
Which you two often agreed upon in the days gone.

APPENDICES

Repetition of the Same Phrases in *Dream of the Rood*

DREAM OF THE ROOD is taken as the earliest manifestation of the literary device commonly referred to as 'dream vision.' Although this view is embraced by most students of Old English literature, in-depth reading of the poem enables us to consider the poem also as a manifesto of literary theory 'enacted'—a work that embodies the critical thought that its author harbored.

The presence of some phrases that repeatedly appear in the poem can be seen as proof of the poet's utilizing oral formulae. But the very fact that the poet employed the same phrases in three distinct stages of the poetic development of the work implies that there was a certain critical consciousness at work while he was composing it. In this essay, I shall try to trace how the poet's critical consciousness may have affected his composition of the poem, even if we grant that many scholars argue for Anglo-Saxon poets' conforming to oral formulae.

The recurrence of the same phrases in different stages of the development of the poem evidences the presence of a stream of consciousness. Although there are two voices in the poem—the dreamer's (or the poet's) and that of the rood personified in his vision—there is unbreakable linkage in its tripartite division. The poem, as a whole, is a marvelous specimen of meta-poetry in the sense that its writer, either consciously or unwittingly, incorporated in his work his critical thought on the inter-relationship between story-telling and listening, ultimately between poetic composition and reading or listening.

There is no question about the Old English poem commonly referred to as *Dream of the Rood* being one of the earliest manifestations of the literary device of resorting to the narrative frame in which the speaker tells what he has undergone in a dream. The poem may be considered the prototype of all the works, in English literature, utilizing this narrative frame, which was a literary convention uniquely medieval.

In reading a poem composed in the narrative frame of dream vision, however, we should remain alert not to take literally what is being uttered by the speaker in it. After all, that narrative frame is only a literary device—but not for truthful confession of what has actually happened in a dream. Then why does a poet resort to the narrative frame of dream vision? Any literary work creative in nature is the record of what its writer has seen and heard in his or her mind's eye and ear. In that respect, any work of imaginative literature can be considered the record of a 'dream vision,' in a broader sense of the phrase. But my present concern is to examine how the poet of this particular poem accomplishes what he wished to accomplish at the outset, by resorting to the narrative frame of dream vision.

The poem consists of three parts. The first twenty-seven lines are an introductory account of the appearance of a vision of the cross, and the voice is the poet's own. Then follows the main body, as well as the major bulk, of the poem (lines 28-121)—the personified cross's telling the dreamer what it underwent throughout the whole process of the Crucifixion. The voice in this central part of the poem is that of the Rood, an inanimate object, yet endowed with individuality and capacity for human ethos and pathos and expression of them through *prosopopoeia*, or personification. The lifeless wood becomes a *reordberend* ('speech-bearer'), so to speak, a kenning, by the way, used twice in the poem (lines 3 and 89) in referring to human beings. The remainder of the poem (lines 122-156) consists of two passages, of which the first (lines

122-148a) is a confession made by the dreamer in regard to the spiritual elevation that the vision has inspired in him, while the second (lines 148b-156) is an allusion to the feelings of the spirits imprisoned at the Harrowing of Hell and to the joy of the angels upon Christ's triumphant return to the heavenly kingdom. As briefly reviewed, in terms of length in its tripartite division, the poem has a symmetrical structure: 27 lines for the introduction of the visionary cross, 94 lines for the visionary cross's narration addressed to the dreamer, and 35 lines for the conclusion.

My attention, however, is drawn, not to the artistic merits or demerits of the poem, but to an aspect of the poem that a careful reader cannot overlook: repetition of certain phrases. One must not consider it simply as a manifestation of oral formulae, much discussed by those who pay attention to the oral nature of Old English poetry. True, a 'literary' or 'lettered' poet could also have utilized the verbal formulae established by their oral predecessors. But to regard repetition of certain phrases observable in an Old English poem simply as a manifestation of oral formulae is tantamount to looking at Old English poetry only as a mass of phrases formed in the oral tradition. When a certain phrase appears more than once in the same poem, a sensitive reader or listener must suspect that some authorial consciousness was at work in the evolution of the poetic lines, whether the poet intended to reveal it or not by so doing. I wish to emphasize how the recurrence of certain phrases in the poem has affected my reading of it. Whether the poet of *Dream of the Rood* would approve of my reception of the work is not my concern, for I strongly believe in what we may call 'the reader's prerogatives.'

The point at issue is not to make a list of the phrases that appear more than once in the poem. My attention is drawn rather to the workings of the authorial consciousness that may have impelled the poet to repeat certain phrases while composing the poem. Did it happen by sheer chance? Or, was there something working in the poet's sub-consciousness that made him do so, but he was not even aware of his so doing? Or, was the poet fully aware of what he was doing, and so he did with full artistic consciousness? Since none can claim that the very process of poetic composition is retraceable, any surmise has to be hypothetical. Nonetheless, I feel strongly inclined to believe that the poet was fully aware of what he was doing, and that he did so for a certain artistic effect he had in mind.

Let us keep in mind the tripartite division of the poem as the basis of our scrutiny on the subject. First, the poet provides the picture of himself having a vision of the Cross. And then, within the picture, which functions as the outermost frame, there is set an inner layer of drawing: the painful experience of being the means of the Crucifixion as recounted by the visionary cross. While reading what the tree tells the dreamer, we, the readers (or, more accurately, the eavesdroppers), partake in the dreamer's experience of listening to the cross's account *and* of re-living the agonizing moments the cross went through during the Crucifixion. When the visionary cross's narration is over, we then hear what effect it has had upon the dreamer, in the concluding passages uttered in the poet's voice again. In this tripartite construction of the poem, certain phrases are being repeated, thus making the listeners correlate the contexts in which they appear.

To rush to my conclusion, the poem as a whole is a manifestation of the poet's attempt to incorporate in a piece of writing his thoughts on the interaction between story-telling and listening—by extension, between the process of poetic composition and the reader's reception of its outcome. To put it bluntly, what we have here in print is a manifesto of literary theory 'enacted'—the poet's thought on the function of imaginative literature being demonstrated within a literary text while its lines evolve. To make my points clear, I argue that *Dream of the Rood* is a work which, partially at least, explores the issue: When a poet attempts poetic creation, what consequences can he expect as an outcome of his effort for artistic creation? Or, to simplify the matter, what is the relationship between writing or reciting, and reading or listening?

The most conspicuous instance of the poet's repeating an identical phrase is found in the verse, 'men ofer moldan, and eall þeos mære gesceaft' ('Men over the earth, and all this glorious creation'):

> Beheoldon þær engel dryhtnes ealle,
> fægere þurh forðgesceaft. Ne wæs ðær huru fracodes gealga,
> ac hine þær beheoldon halige gastas,
> *men ofer moldan, ond eall þeos mære gesceaft.* (9b-12)

[All the Lord's angels, beautiful by creation,
Looked on there. That was indeed not a gallows for a felon,
For the holy spirits looked on it there, as
Men over the earth and all this glorious creation did.]

Bruce Mitchell and Fred C. Robinson read lines 9b-10a as follows:

> Behēoldon þǣr *engel* Dryhtnes ealle
> fægere þurh forðgesceaft; (9b-10a)

And their interpretation of the above is:

> "All those fair by eternal decree gazed on the angel of the Lord (i.e. Christ or possibly the cross) there." (Bruce Mitchell and Fred C. Robinson, *A Guide to Old English*, 6th edition, Oxforf: Blackwell, 2001, p. 258, note on 9b-10a)

Mitchell and Robinson misread the lines. Although they correctly add that "'those fair by eternal decree' are the *hālige gāstas* (line 11)—the loyal angels who were predestined to remain in Heaven" (Mitchell and Robinson, p. 258, note), they miss the point: the whole creation, including the blessed angels chosen to be the 'halige gastas' (line 11), was looking on the Cross. The emphasis here is that the bright Rood in the poet's vision is magnetically drawing the attention of the whole creation, including the blessed angels: hence, 'men over the earth and all this glorious creation' (line 12).

The second time when the phrase—'men ofer moldan, and eall þeos mære gesceaft'—appears is on line 82:

'Nu ðu miht gehyran, hæleð min se leofa,
þæt ic bealuwa weorc gebiden hæbbe,
sarra sorga. Is nu sæl cumen
þæt me weorðiað wide ond side
men ofer moldan, ond eall þeos mære gesceaft,
gebiddað him to þyssum beacne. (78-83a)

['Now you can hear, my dear man,
That I have endured what the evil-doers did,
Work of painful sorrows. Now is the time come
That they honor me far and wide—
Men over the earth, and all this glorious creation—
Pray to this beacon.]

Why does the phrase, which, by the way, constitutes an entire line, have to appear twice in the same poem? Should we regard it merely as a coincidence, or as another instance of the manifestation of oral formulae, or as something intentionally done by the poet? The fact that the rather long phrase made up of eight words ('men ofer moldan, and eall þeos mære gesceaft') appears in two different stages of poetic development—once in the introductory part of the poem, in which the first-person narrator on the outermost layer, the poet, tells us how he encountered a vision, and again within the utterance of the personified cross in the poet's vision—makes us scrutinize on a possible link between the outer layer of the poem and the core of the work, the narration of the cross.

The juxtaposition of two identical lines appearing in two different stages of poetic development—first, in the introductory part depicting the epiphany of the Cross, and then in the visionary cross's message to the dreamer—suggests interaction between the poetic situations set up in the two parts. Whether the poet intended it or not, doubtless there is not only verbal resonance but a stream of consciousness running through the two phases of poesy-making. In the dreamer's vision, 'Men over the earth, and this glorious creation' (line 12) looked on the Rood; now the visionary cross, in its address to the dreamer, demands that 'Men over the earth, and all this glorious creation' (line 82) pray to the beacon. Another attention-calling instance is found in the recurrence of the phrase, 'elne mycle' ('with great zeal'). This phrase appears three times in the poem: lines 34, 60, and 123. The first time it appears is when the visionary cross tells the dreamer how eager Christ was to mount on the rood:

'Geseah ic þa frean mancynnes
efstan *elne mycle* þæt he me wolde on gestigan. (33b–34)

['Then I saw the Lord of mankind
Hasten *with great zeal*, for He wished to mount on me.]

The second time the phrase appears is when the cross tells the dreamer how much it felt inclined to cooperate with those who had come from afar to take care of Christ's body after the Crucifixion:

Hwæðere þær fuse feorran cwoman
to þam æðelinge. Ic þæt eall beheold.
Sare ic wæs mid sorgum gedrefed, hnag ic hwæðre þam
secgum to handa,
eaðmod *elne mycle*. (57–60a)

[However, there came the eager ones in haste from afar
To the Prince; I beheld that all. I was in pain,
Afflicted with sorrows; I stooped, however, to the hands
of the men,
Humble, with great zeal.]

The third and the last time the phrase appears is when, after the visionary cross's recount is over, the dreamer tells us how much he has been reformed by the vision and is now prepared to worship the Cross without any shade of doubt or skepticism:

Gebæd ic me þa to þan beame bliðe mode,
elne mycle, þær ic ana wæs
mæte werede. Wæs modsefa
afysed on forðwege, feala ealra gebad
langunghwila. (122–126a)

[Then I prayed to the cross in glad cheer,
With great zeal, where I was alone,
With no company. My soul was
Urged on forth away; I endured many bouts
Of longing.]

I don't think reiteration of the phrase 'elne mycle' in the above three passages is haphazard. There is a kind of chain reaction felt passage after passage. In its address to the dreamer, the cross says that Christ mounted on the gallows 'with great zeal' for redemption of mankind (33b-34); then, when those who had come from afar to take care of the body of Christ were trying to lower it from the gallows, the cross says, it 'stooped to [their] hands. . . , humble, *with great zeal*' (59b-60a). Telling the dreamer how it felt when the Crucifixion was going on, the cross has said: 'I did not dare then, against the Lord's word, bend or burst, when I saw the surface of the earth tremble. I could have crushed all my enemies; nevertheless, I stood fast' (35-38); 'I trembled when the Man embraced me; yet I did not dare to bend to earth, fall to the surface of the earth, but I had to stand fast' (42-43); 'I was raised to be the Rood; I heaved the powerful King, Lord of the heavens. I did not dare to bow down.' (44-45) Then, why suddenly the picture of the cross stooping to cooperate with those who were trying to lower Christ's body?

Earlier in its recounting of the Crucifixion, the Rood tells the dreamer at one point:

Þurhdrifan hi me mid deorcan næglum. On me syndon
   þa dolg gesiene,
opene inwidhlemmas. Ne dorste ic hira nænigum sceððan.
Bysmeredon hie *unc butu ætgædere.* (46-48a)

[They pierced me with dark nails; on me are the wounds seen,
Open, malicious wounds; nor did I dare injure any of them.
They mocked *us both together.*]

'Us both together'—when the cross says so, the implication is that union, or fusion, of the two—the cross and Christ—was complete at the moment of nail-hammering. Insomuch as the cross's self-identification with Christ had been attained, it had to feel and act exactly as Christ did. Hence the cross's being willing to '[stoop] to the hands of the men, humble, *with great zeal.*'

I will cite one more case of an identical phrase appearing more than once. One might argue that the phrase in question is simply an instance of understatement: 'mæte weorode' (literally, 'with little company,' meaning 'alone'). The phrase first appears in the passage where the visionary cross tells the dreamer how 'the eager ones' (implied by the word 'fuse' on line 57), who had come from afar to retrieve the body of Christ, built a tomb and, after placing Corpus Christi therein, took their journey back, leaving Him behind alone:

> Ongunnon him þa sorhleoð galan
> earme on þa æfentide, þa hie woldon eft siðian,
> meðe fram þam mæran þeodne. Reste he ðær
> *mæte weorode.* (67b-69)

> [Then they began to sing Him a dirge,
> The miserable ones, in the eventide, when they
> would travel back,
> Weary, from the glorious Prince. He rested there
> *with no company.*]

The phrase 'mæte weorode' reappears later in the poem, with a slightly different spelling ('mæte werede'), when the poet tells us how, after listening to what the visionary cross has said to him, he finds himself reformed and ready to commit himself to worship of the Rood:

> Gebæd ic me þa to þan beame bliðe mode,
> elne mycle, þær ic ana wæs
> *mæte werede.* Wæs modsefa
> afysed on forðwege, feala ealra gebad
> langunghwila. (122-126a)

[Then I prayed to the cross in glad cheer,
With great zeal, where I was alone,
With no company. My soul was
Urged on forth away; I endured many bouts
Of longing.]

This passage has already been quoted earlier, as an illustration of repeating the phrase 'elne mycle.' I quote the passage again for the purpose of pointing out that the reappearance of the phrase 'mæte weorode' (69), with a slightly different spelling, 'mæte werede' (124), which smacks of rather common Germanic understatement, somehow suggests a possible link between its first appearance in the passage depicting Christ being left alone in his tomb, and its reappearance in the passage depicting the poet being left alone only with the lingering image of the Rood after the vision.

Just as the cross went through the process of undergoing change, not merely physical but spiritual, as indicated in its recount of the whole sequence of the events involving the Crucifixion—being chopped off in a wood, being carried to Golgotha to stand as a gallows, bearing Corpus Christi, having been pierced by the same nails as driven through Christ's body, witnessing the lowering of Corpus Christi that was to be entombed, being left deserted on Golgotha in the dark, being buried in a deep pit ('Bedealf us man on deopan seaþe') (75), and finally being excavated by Christ's disciples to be extolled as the emblem of Christ's glory—so did the dreamer undergo spiritual regeneration. The body of Christ had to be left alone in His tomb newly delved: 'Reste he ðær mæte weorode' ('He rested there *with no company*') (69). Now that the dreamer had heard all the recount of the cross, he could somehow get closer to understanding the loneliness Christ must have felt while going through the Passion. For that reason, the dreamer could '[pray] to the cross in glad cheer, *with great zeal,* where [he] was alone, *with no company*' (122-124a).

The verbal echoes traceable here and there in the poem, as examined above, signify a certain continuity of the flow of consciousness. The tripartite division of the poem notwithstanding, each segment is linked to the others, not only structurally but in terms of the stream of consciousness. And that flow is implied by reiteration of the same words and phrases. The first-person narrator in the outermost layer, while telling us about his having had a vision of the Cross, says:

> Hwæðre ic þurh þæt gold ongytan meahte
> earmra ærgewin, þæt hit ærest ongan
> swætan on þa swiðran healfe. Eall ic wæs *mid sorgum gedrefed*,
> (18–20)

> [Nevertheless I could perceive through that gold
> The bygone strife of the miserable, see that it first began to
> Bleed on the right side. I was entirely *afflicted with sorrow*;]

The dreamer, while watching the bleeding wounds on the right side of the cross—by extension, on the right side of Christ's body—was 'entirely *afflicted with sorrow.*' And, the cross tells the dreamer in its recount that, when 'the eager ones' came to retrieve Corpus Christi, it 'was in pain, *afflicted with sorrow*':

> Hwæðere þær fuse feorran cwoman
> to þam æðelinge. Ic þæ eall beheold.
> Sare ic wæs *mid sorgum gedrefed*, hnag ic hwæðre þam
> secgum to handa,
> eaðmod elne mycle. (57–60a)

> [However, there came the eager ones in haste from afar
> To the Prince; I beheld that all. I was in pain,
> *Afflicted with sorrow*; I stooped, however, to the hands
> of the men,
> Humble, with great zeal.]

As much as the wounds received by Christ are felt poignantly by the wooden cross, so the dreamer, who has heard the recount made by the cross, can relive the moments of the painful suffering both of Christ and the Cross. This is what the poem is all about—the power of telling a story, or of making a confession. In a distinct way, *Dream of the Rood* is a manifestation of what the modern literary theorists have termed 'meta-poetry.'

It is a poem not only about the sublime moment of epiphany of the divine glory, but also about how a chain reaction is bound to occur when the process of telling a story and listening to it goes on—which is what literature is all about. How the dreamer, the listener of the visionary cross's narration, has been transformed is being shown toward the end of *Dream of the Rood*. The real essence of the artistry of the poem, after all, does not lie in what we read line after line, but in the overall picture of a man being transformed—being assimilated with the story-teller—as the poem progresses, while a gradual buildup of sentiments in the readers' consciousness coincides with what develops in the poet's own as he writes on.

The Speaker in *The Lament of an Outcast* (or *The Wife's Lament*)

ALL THE TITLES OF the Old English poems known to modern-day readers have been assigned by scholars who based their denomination of each poem on its overall content. The practice has been a matter of convenience, and, it is true, literary discussion of Old English poetry has been facilitated by the existence of commonly accepted titles. Since an arbitrarily assigned title is bound to influence the readers' reception of a given work, however, we cannot always retain positive feelings about the way the title of a work affects our interpretation of the lines we read. Preconception of a work arising from its given title can lead us to a wrong interpretation of the work as a whole or of certain passages or phrases. Once the overall picture of a work imposed on it by its title has been embedded in our consciousness, it is hard for us to be free from its influence; and quite often, without realizing it, we perpetrate the blunder of trying to read a work within a pre-conceived mold of interpretation. What happens is comparable to putting on a pair of glasses of certain color, or wearing a visor that allows one to see things only within the scope permitted.

The Old English poem commonly referred to as "The Wife's Lament" is typical of the case in which a conveniently assigned title has set the boundary of the meaning of a poem. In order for us to figure out what the poem is all about, we must read the lines with fresh eyes, remaining ever receptive to what they tell us. Before presenting my argument on the theme and the narrative frame of the poem as I see it, I propose that the readers of this essay take another look at the whole text of the poem in my Modern English translation.

One can easily construe that the poem concerns itself with the alienation of the first-person narrator—up to line 41—from his or her lord and the ensuing pain of loneliness and dejection from which the speaker suffers. The commonly accepted title of the poem, "The Wife's Lament" (or its variant, "The Maiden's Complaint") is grounded on the fact that the very first sentence of the poem contains three subsequent words with feminine ending:

> Ic þis giedd wrece bi me ful *geomorre,*
> *minre sylfre* sið. (1–2a)

The feminine endings of the adjective 'geomorre' and the first-person pronoun phrase 'minre sylfre' have provided ground for assuming that the speaker in the poem is a woman. But this assumption based on grammatical manifestation in the text has been in collision with the overall content of the poem. To begin with, one can hardly expect to encounter a poem in Old English supposedly delivered in female voice. The minstrel reciting a poem in a mead-hall, without exception, was a man. Then what is going on here?

Several different hypothetical explanations have been provided by scholarly ingenuity, ranging from the conjecture that the scribe who left the extant manuscript of the poem may have made a blunder in transcribing the three words, thus resulting in writing down feminine endings for them to the suggestion that the extant text could be a fragment of a work whose entirety would clearly explain the context in which the lament appears. Any conjecture on the changes that may have occurred in the transmission of the text of a work is permissible. But one fundamental principle should remain unchallenged: the principle that one must try to make the most of the extant text of a work, whether it really is a fragment or may contain scribal errors. Whatever has been transmitted to posterity in the form of a manuscript should be treated as a complete and accurate text, unless it is a case like that of "The Ruin," the extant text of which clearly proves itself to be fragmentary. All our effort toward imaginative reading and interpretation of a work should be allowed within the boundary set by its surviving text. I do not wish to recapitulate here all the interpretations provided by earlier Old English scholars. It would be an attempt irrelevant to the purpose of this essay. I only wish to write down what I have personally gathered while reading the poem.

Each fresh attempt to read an Old English poem should begin with imaginary partaking of the poetic situation in which it was being recited by a minstrel. As we start to read the poem in question, we must first hear the twang of the minstrel's harp in our mind's ear; and then the first sentence is uttered:

> I sing this song about myself in deep sorrow
> By telling what I have undergone. (1–2a)

No matter how we may wish to approach the poem as a written document, one undeniable fact is that the audience, who listened to the minstrel's recitation, was a group of men, including the chieftain (whether a king or the head of a tribe) and his retainers. In view of this uniquely male-oriented poetic situation, it is only natural to surmise that the theme of a poem being recited had to concern itself with a topic to which the audience would easily respond. The minstrel, of course, is not a man-at-arms; but he knows too well the lives of the Anglo-Saxon retainers. He could be a wandering poet who, having witnessed what happened to a tribe, utilized the story in his verbal entertainment for other tribes; or he could be someone who, as in the case of the speaker in "The Wanderer," had personally undergone a painful journey in search of another ring-giver. In any case, the poem being recited in the mead-hall had to touch the heartstrings of the listeners by having some affinity with their own personal experiences.

Let us envision a mead-hall filled with men who have taken it as the summit of their lives to die in battle for the glory of their clansmen, thereby fulfilling their pledge to the code of *comitatus*.

After the first twang of the minstrel's harp, there follows a lament, the implied speaker of which is unquestionably a woman, as the feminine endings of the few words mentioned above make it clear. The minstrel is a man; but the fictional character who utters the lament through the minstrel's voice is obviously a woman. How can we reconcile the two incompatible facts? In reading an Old English poem, one must take into consideration that its intended audience was well trained in the aural perception of the lines orally delivered. Without providing any introductory note on the speaker of the lament, the minstrel starts his recitation. His audience, being a well-trained one, instantly detects that the utterances delivered in the voice of a woman are meant to be a transfiguration of what can come out of the mouth of an alienated and ostracized retainer when his tie of *comitatus* is broken. By beginning his poem with a sentence implying that the speaker is a woman, the minstrel captures his audience's attention.

Having made the audience aware that the speaker is in a state of unrelieved pain and loneliness in the first five lines, the poem moves along to mention the incident that was the beginning of the speaker's present misery:

> First, my lord departed hence from his people
> Over the turbulent wave; at each dawn I grieved,
> Wondering where my lord on earth would be.
> Then I, a forlorn wretch, unable to bear my woe,
> Set out on a journey in search of my service. (6-10)

The lord left the speaker behind, thus initiating the separation between them. Whatever the reason for the lord's departure from his people, the speaker could not accompany him. The two lines (9-10), however, pose a problem:

> Then I, a forlorn wretch, unable to bear my woe,
> Set out on a journey in search of my service. (9-10)

Does the sentence mean that the speaker embarked on a journey in search of another lord to serve, as in the case of the speaker in "The Wanderer," or to join the lord who excluded the speaker from the band to accompany him on his voyage? If the former was the case, it presupposes the lord's death, for it is an act of betrayal to look for another one to serve while the lord is still alive. So, was the latter the case? And if the speaker is a woman, indeed, it just does not make much sense. One can hardly imagine that the wife of a man, whose social status is apparently no lower than that of the leader of a tribe, could embark on a solitary journey in search of her husband. The most plausible interpretation, then, is that the speaker of the lament—apparently a woman, in voice—is a metaphorical figure that stands for a man excluded from the group in his lord's favor.

The poem continues:

> My man's kinsfolk began to conspire
> In a dark plan to separate us two,
> So that we would be far apart in this world
> And live in great misery—and my heart ached.
> My lord ordered me to dwell here;
> I have none of my dear ones, in this part of the world,
> Not one of my faithful friends. So my heart is heavy
> To perceive that the man most companionable to me,
> Stricken by ill luck, sad in heart,
> Hiding his deep thought, even contemplates my death.
> Joyfully we would often swear
> That nothing but death would sever us two;
> All that has turned the other way round;
> It is now as if it had never been—
> Love of ours. Far and near I must endure
> The hatred my dear one harbors toward me. (11-26)

We may read the above passage in two different ways. It can mean that the speaker, after making a solitary journey to join the lord, finally attained reunion with him, only to become an object of his hostility as a consequence of his kinsmen's conspiracy to banish the speaker from his favor. The other possibility is that the passage can be read as an explanatory note on the circumstance that has already been mentioned in the preceding lines. The question is whether what is told in the above passage happened after the speaker's solitary voyage, or whether it is an elaboration on the circumstance that has already been mentioned. Personally, I prefer the latter reading. The poetic form of dramatic monologue does not follow the sequence of the events; it rather takes the liberty of stating whatever looms in the speaker's consciousness, without following the chronological order. Whichever the case may be, what is being emphasized in the above passage is the fact that the pledge of lifelong mutual love between the lord and the speaker has been shattered by the conspiracy of those near the former.

Suppose the speaker is not a metaphor of a retainer alienated from his lord but is a woman, indeed. Then one question arises: Was the conjugal relationship between a woman and her husband so crucially important for the man's relatives as to necessitate their conspiracy to separate them? Of course, even in a warrior society, a trivial domestic issue could have led a man's relatives to attempt to put an end to his marital relationship. But in view of the cultural climate of the Teutonic warrior society, we can hardly imagine that such familial trouble could have been the subject of a poem to be recited in a mead-hall. A story such as, say, that of Othello killing Desdemona, instigated by the treachery of Iago, could become the subject of a literary work in a much later age; it hardly could have been a subject matter in Old English poetry. What is told in "The Wife's Lament" in the guise of a marital breakup, then, should be taken as a metaphor. In any society, envy and jealousy exist. We have known innumerable cases of the breakup of the bond between a king and his beloved subject, caused by political intrigue and conspiracy of those who were jealous of their closeness. And such a case can be narrated metaphorically in terms of the breakup of a conjugal tie.

In the passage quoted above, there are a couple of phrases that call our attention: "þurh dyrne geþoht" ("through dark thought," i.e. "in a dark plan") (12) and "mod miþendne, morþor hycgendne" ("hiding his thought, contemplating murder") (20). What is implied in these phrases is that the circumstance being told in the poem has more to do with a political situation than with a simple familial breakup caused by misunderstanding or cooling off of love-passion. There have been innumerable cases in human history, both in the East and in the West, of the breakup of the bond between a king and his loyal subject, initiated by those who are jealous of the latter. In several such cases, an indicted subject had to be put in exile or be executed, quite against the will of his liege-lord. The line, "mod miþendne, morþor hycgendne" ("hiding his thought, contemplating murder") (20), is an accurate description of the dilemma into which the speaker's lord was put: the lord still loves the one who utters the lament, but is torn between his love for the latter and the painful task imposed on him publicly—which is to execute him. And the one who utters the lament knows too well what sort of pain his beloved lord is going through. The last sentence in the passage quoted above sounds meaningful: "Sceal ic feor ge neah / mines felaleofan fæhðu dreogan" ("Far and near must I endure the hatred my dear man harbors toward me") (25b-26). One of the most prevailing themes in Old English poetry, *Sic transit Gloria mundi*, after all, does not apply only to the vicissitude of a kingdom or to the rise and fall of the fortune of a warrior. That human emotions, such as love, can undergo change in the flow of time is manifested in these lines.

The ensuing passage of the poem (27-41) contains a few important points to be taken into consideration. The speaker was ordered to live in complete isolation. Moreover, the place assigned as the speaker's dwelling is "under an oak tree, in a cave dug in the earth" (28). Why "under an oak tree, in a cave dug in the earth"? What special meaning can be attached to the "an oak tree"? What about the "cave dug in the earth"? Sunlight is blocked from the "cave dug in the earth," and the dweller therein is completely segregated from human society. I wonder if an oak tree had any implication related to shamanism in Old Germanic culture. And if the speaker's assigned dwelling is such a bleak place, it can mean death, not physical, but spiritual. The punishment given to the speaker is more spiritual than physical, in the sense that despair arising from complete isolation is its outcome. And the speaker employs the metaphor of the dark cave in a deep mountain to emphasize spiritual devastation. Suppose the speaker is a woman who has committed a heinous deed. Would it be possible to put her, the wife of a king, or at least of the leader of a clan, in exile of such extremity, unless she happens to be a victim of a dreadfully contagious disease? The earth-cave under an oak tree must be symbolic of the spiritual inferno in which the speaker is put. Another attention-calling part in the above passage is the speaker's alluding to loss of bed-right in conjugal life: "In this world / Lovers are, who live together, sharing the same bed, / When I all alone walk at dawn / Under the oak tree, crossing the earth-cave" (33b-36). Here we do not have to take the phrase, "sharing the same bed" literally. With the presupposition that the poem is a lament uttered by a woman rejected by her husband—a hypothetical poetic situation imposed by the minstrel on his audience—it is only natural that lines on deprivation of bed-right appear. But we may as well read the complaint as a metaphor, not literally.

I firmly believe that the lament of the fictional speaker ends with line 41. The ensuing lines (42-53) are not continuation of the lament uttered in the voice of the fictional speaker but a sort of afterthought that the poet utters in his own voice. The same minstrel carries on recitation; but, without telling his audience that the fictional complainer's lament is over, the poet (or the minstrel) switches to his own voice and provides concluding words on the suffering of the one who has uttered a lament up to that point:

> The young man must ever be in grief,
> His thought drenched in sorrow, while he must keep
> A cheerful bearing, despite his breast's pain
> And sorrow thronging endlessly. All his worldly joy
> Will depend on him, though he may be banished far
> To live in exile in a distant land; my friend sits
> Under a rocky slope, frost-bit in storm,
> My weary-hearted friend, drenched with rain,
> In his dreary dwelling place. My friend endures
> Great pain and grief; he often recalls
> A dwelling more replenished with joy. Woe be with him
> Who must wait for his beloved man with longing. (42-53)

My reading of these lines, which conclude the poem, differs from what some scholars think of them. They take the lines as continuation of the complaint uttered by the first-person narrator. A preposterous interpretation of the passage arising from this reading is that the rejected 'woman' finds consolation in the thought that her husband, who has banished her, will also suffer from longing for her.[1] Despite the weight that observations made by the prominent scholars should carry along with them, I simply cannot concur with them in believing that the poet ended the lament by casting a tinge of the thought that "misery loves company." If the complainer's last source for relief from pain is the belief that the rejected speaker's lord also must be suffering from the pain of separation, then it goes directly against the spirit of stoical endurance that all Old English poetry embraces.

What calls our attention is the fact that the first-person pronoun 'ic' does not appear in the concluding passage of the poem. Instead, phrases alluding to a third person, such as "geong mon" (42), "min freond" (47), and "min wine" (50), appear; and the third-person pronoun 'he' (51) finally appears at the very end of the poem. Do all these refer to the husband who has rejected his wife? The speaker of the lament has used phrases, such as "min hlaford" (6), "min leodfruma" (8), "hlaford min" (15), "frean" (33), and so forth, in referring to the one who is the object of longing. If the concluding passage of the poem is continuation of the lament, are there any reasons why the appellations of the speaker's lord should suddenly switch to such friendly terms as "geong mon," "min freond," and "min wine"?

---

1. "The final section (ll. 42–53) seems to be the wife's speculations as to the husband's present circumstances and her assurances to herself that he must feel as sad as she when he recalls their former life together. She closes with a gnomic observation about the suffering of parted lovers." (Bruce Mitchell and Fred C. Robinson, ed. *A Guide to Old English*, Oxford: Blackwell, 1986, p. 248.) On the same lines Mitchell and Robinson added in a footnote: "Here the speaker seems to speculate over what might be the present state of her estranged spouse and to assure herself that whatever his circumstances he will certainly be sharing her sorrow over their separation." (The same book, p. 250)

My belief is that the allusions to a third person—"geong mon" (42), "min freond" (47), "min wine" (50), and "he" (51)—all allude to that very person who has so far uttered the lament, not the man who has banished the speaker, thereby causing much pain for the latter. The minstrel, up to the end of line 41, has recited the lament of a fictional speaker who has been estranged from the one who is the object of longing; and so far the assumed voice has been that of a woman. But from line 42, which begins with a fresh twang of his harp, the minstrel (or the poet) sings in *his* own voice: the speaker of the concluding lines (42-53) is not the fictional person in mourning but the poet himself. We find a similar change of voice in "The Wanderer" toward the end of the poem. As the poem reaches its end, the poet, who has uttered a monologue in the voice of a wanderer, returns to his own voice and concludes the poem by providing his comment on the dramatic monologue he has so far recited:

> So spoke the wise man, and sat apart in meditation.
> Good is he who holds his pledge: a man must never
>   too hastily release
> His indignation out of his breast, unless he knows
>   beforehand the remedy
> A man can perform with fortitude. Well is it for
>   him who seeks mercy for himself,
> Comfort from Father in the heavens, where stands
>   security for us all.
> (*The Wanderer*, 111-115)

The concluding line of *The Wife's Lament* (or rather, *The Lament of an Outcast*) also should be read as a passage containing a didactic message, the way the closure of *The Wanderer* contains the poet's moralization.

Having figuratively shown the sadness of a young retainer estranged from his ring-giver by borrowing mournful utterances of a banished wife, the poet now releases his audience from the fictional situation he has set up, and moralizes on the predicament that men must face when *comitatus*, the foundation of human interaction in the male-oriented Anglo-Saxon society, is broken. And what is being emphasized in the last dozen of lines is the nobility of the spirit of stoical endurance in the presence of the pain that life can bring, whether it be that of a breakup of friendship or of a conjugal relationship. The third-person references appearing in the concluding passage (42-53)—"geong mon," "min freond," "min wine," and "he"—all allude to the first-person speaker of the lament, which the minstrel has recited up to line 41. The first-person pronoun "ic" has been heard so many times while the speaker's lament goes on. But in the concluding lines it is no longer heard. The two instances of the use of "min" (47 and 50) and the genitive-case form of the first-person pronoun "ic" refer to the poet, or the minstrel, not the first-person narrator of the preceding lament.

The pain of estrangement and separation can come to anyone's life. Although the third-person references—"geong mon," "min freond," "min wine," and "he"—allude to the specific fictional character who has uttered a lament, they loom as words denoting an Everyman figure: each man listening to the lament, sitting in a mead-hall, could have identified himself with the luckless young man who laments his estrangement from his ring-giver, for it can happen to any man at any time in his life. What really matters in life is the courage to embrace the pain and and sorrow that life may inflict on us—the spirit of stoical endurance and manly fortitude, a theme that runs throughout Old English poetry. This is what the poet emphasizes in the twelve lines—in *his* own voice.

When we read an Old English poem, we must always keep in mind the 'dramatic' situation a minstrel was in, as a performing artist. Old English poetry was meant for oral delivery and aural reception, not for ocular reading. And it required a sort of an 'actor,' who was expected to recite the lines in the right tone and voice, accompanied by appropriate facial expressions and bodily movement. A literary setting for Old English poetry is thus conceivable only when its three requirements are met: the poet, who composed the lines; the minstrel, who recited them; and the audience, who listened to the recitation, although the poet and the minstrel, the 'scop' ('creator'), often could have been the same person. With high theatricality as its main attribute, Old English poetry thus had to contain a complex array of dramatic voices.

The Convergence of the Content and the State of the Manuscript of *The Ruin*

THE PRESENT CONDITION OF the manuscript of the poetic fragment contained in the Exeter Book, often referred to as "The Ruin," does not allow us even to guess how long the poem was. Arranged in verse after prosodic scheme, the text is clear up to line 12; the ensuing six lines are undecipherable. With the off-verse of line 18, the work resumes textual clarity, till it reaches the on-verse of line 42, after which the manuscript becomes illegible again. The condition in which the manuscript has been preserved is such that one cannot even presume how long the poem initially was or what the rest of the work was about. The common appellation of the work, "The Ruin," is based on the content of the extant text of the work, of course; but this title ironically becomes applicable to the state in which the work has been preserved.

Although it is impossible to envision the original shape of the poem, the extant thirty-eight lines, which are decipherable, provide enough suggestion as to the overall tenor of the work. The theme of the poem is the much too recurrent thought geared to 'Ubi sunt qui ante nos fuerunt' and 'Sic transit gloria mundi.' One of the most recurrent motifs in Old English poetry is *dust-sceawung* ('contemplation of the dust'), the core of which is the thought that all existing things, including men and women, will eventually turn into dust. This motif is a ubiquitous one in Old English poetry; but "The Ruin" is a unique case, for the whole poem seems to have been composed to emphasize this theme. The first twelve lines read:

> Wondrous is this stone-wall; yet Fate has demolished
> The fortress—so the giants' work crumbles.
> Roofs are fallen off, towers have fallen down,
> Rusty doors broken, frost fills the gap between stones,
> The walls that fended off the stormy wind and snow
> Are cracked, and crumble in the flow of time.
> The masons who died long ago
> Are lying, confined in the cold ground, while
> A hundred generations have flowed with time.
> The stonewalls, gray with moss and reddened with rust,
> Have withstood the storm and snow,
> Witnessing the kingdoms' rise and fall;
> Though high and wide, they have also fallen down.
> Yet, torn and burst by rain and wind,
> The art of masonry lives on in this work.
> (My translation)

What is being emphasized in these opening lines is the power of fate (*wyrd*) that turns whatever man can attain—no matter of what grandeur it may be—into dust. The first word in the first line is 'wrætlic' ('wonderful' or 'wondrous'). The wonder that the poet feels is not only that about the grandeur of the stone-wall that overwhelms an onlooker. The strong message conveyed to the listener in the first line—"Wrætlic is þes wealstan; wyrde gebræcon"—containing a series of *w*-alliteration—is the power of fate that has turned the grand stone-wall into a ruin. The crumbling stones, however, still retain the trace of the art of masonry that has survived the flow of time tyrannized over by fate; therefore, they are 'wondrous.'

What is being emphasized in the poem is not only the present state of decay that the poet is witnessing. By allowing the readers (or the listeners) to envision the prosperity and grandeur of the past that lies hidden behind the present scene of bleakness, the poem makes the transience of all worldly glory and pomp even more poignantly felt. For this reason, the work provides a kind of rhythm—the alternation of the present state of decay and the prosperity of the past that the reader can see in his mind's eye as the poem progresses. In the passage quoted above, there are lines that call the reader's attention:

> Earth-grip has
> The master-builders perished and gone—
> The hard grip of the earth has—till a hundred generations
> Of people have passed; often this wall has experienced
> Gray with moss, and reddened with rust, kingdom after kingdom,
> Enduring under storms; high and wide, it has collapsed.
> Yet the wall-stone remains, though gashed by weather....
> (ll. 6-12)

Just as the manuscript of the poem is in such a poor state of preservation that one can hardly envision its original shape, so is the picture drawn by the poet bleak and dreary to the utmost degree. But the poet clearly says: Although the masons who built the tall fortress have long since turned into dust, and their work has long since turned into a pile of stones, their craftsmanship still lives on in the ruins of their artifact. We see an instance of metapoetry, though the poet may not have intended it. The work continues, after the ensuing five lines and a half, which are undecipherable:

> wove together into the rings
> A swift ingenuity, and the resolute one bound
> The wall-braces with wires wonderfully together;
> Bright were the fortresses; there were many bathing halls,
> A high abundance of gables; great noise of an army,
> Many a mead-hall full of the joys of men,
> Till Fate changed all that utterly;
> The slaughtered men fell far and wide; the days of pestilence came,
> Death took all of the brave men;

Their places of worship became deserted,
And the town decayed. The menders of the buildings died,
The pagan sanctuaries in earth; therefore, the buildings
grow desolate,
And the red curved roof parts from the tiles
Of the ceiling vault; ruin swept the ground,
Shattered to mounds of stone, where once many a man,
Joyful and bright with gold, adorned with splendor,
Shone with war trappings, proud and wine-flushed;
They cast their eyes on treasure, on silver, on precious stones,
On wealth, on property, on jewelry,
In the bright town of the expansive kingdom; (ll. 18b-37)

In line 12, the poet wrote: "Wunað giet se wealstan wede-rum geheawen," ("Yet, torn and burst by rain and wind, the art of masonry lives on in this wreck"). Although the ensuing five or six lines are undecipherable, the words appearing in the next three lines (from the off-verse of line 18 to the off-verse of line 20) supplement what the poet has said in line 12:

swiftne gebrægd
hwætred in hringas, hygerof gebond
weallwalan wirum wundrum togædre.

[the wondrous shapes
They engraved within circles, and with firm intention
Bound the stones with iron chains.]

What the poet sees now is only a ruin. But the poet's thought hovers between the past and the present, and his lines evolve, while the prosperity of the past and the decay of the present run in parallel. When the poet witnesses the present decay, it means that his mind's eye, at the same time, can see the prosperity of the past, which must have preceded it. Now, where will this development of the poetic imagination lead the poet? While witnessing the scene of the present decay—the remnant of the past prosperity—the poet comes to realize the horrible truth—that his present self and those who share the bliss of being alive with him—like the warriors and the masons who have left only the piles of stones behind—who *did* pursue glory and fame in their own way—will eventually turn into dust. Not the "present-ness of the present," but "the past-ness of the present," which will come in time—this is what the poet must face as truth. And it is also the truth *we* must realize while reading this poem entitled "The Ruin," the manuscript of which remains in a state of ruin.

The last lines of the work are almost undecipherable, like the case of lines 13-18; yet the five or six lines that follow the lines quoted above (ll. 18b-37) are clear enough for us to construe their meaning, and provoke the readers to exert their imagination:

> Stanhofu stodan, stream hate wearp
> widan wylme; weal eall befeng
> beorhtan bosme, þær þa baþu wæron,
> hat on hreþre. Þæt wæs hyðelic.
> Leton þonne geotan [. . . . .]
> ofer harne stan hate streamas (ll. 38-43)

> [Here stood the buildings made of stones,
> And the hot spring must have flowed,
> While in the middle of the walls surrounding
> Hot spring water must have overflowed.
> What pleasure would it have been!
> Hot stream must have flowed over the ashen stones. . . .]

Scholars guess that the poem reveals what the poet felt while visiting a ruin in Bath, a hot spring town believed to have been built by the Romans in the remote past, long before the Anglo-Saxons came to the island to settle. But what difference does it make, whether it be true or not? What matters is the fact that the work still survives, even in fragment, and makes us indulge in this thought: "On this crumbling piece of sheep-skin must have flowed the lines of a poet. They must have been splendid lines—that ran on as if in a carefree stream. . . ." As if to justify our indulging in the thought, "The Ruin" stops in line 49, leaving five or six lines behind, which fade away in undecipherable words. Though not intended by the poet, the content of the poem and the state in which it has been preserved converge.

Is the Sender of the Message in *The Husband's Message* a 'Husband'?

THE TITLE THAT SCHOLARS have assigned to a poem or a poetic fragment on the basis of its apparent overall content can often mislead the readers by confining their reception of the work within the boundary of interpretation implied by it. There is no absolute guarantee that the title scholars have assigned to a poem or a poetic fragment is one that accurately captures its real substance. As a matter of fact, it involves much risk to confine or define the implication of a literary piece by assigning a title on the basis of its apparent content—'apparent' only on its surface level.

There is an Old English poetic fragment often referred to as "The Husband's Message." Its extant manuscript is in such a state of ruin that, despite the legibility of some words, its opening lines do not provide any clue to the poetic situation of the fragment. It is only with the off-verse of the fifth line, as lineated in accordance with Old English prosody, that the lines begin to make any sense:

> Ful oft ic on bates
> [. . . . .] gesohte
> þær mec mondryhten min [. . . . . .]
> ofer heah hofu; eom nu her cumen
> on ceolþele, ond nu cunnan scealt
> hu þu ymb modlufan mines frean

on hyge hycge. Ic gehatan dear
þæt þu þær tirfæste treowe findest. (5b-12)

[Full often in the bosom
Of a boat I . . . .   sought,
Where my liege lord . . .   me . . . .
Over the high seas; I have now come here
In a ship, and now you shall know
How concerning the heart's love of my lord
You should think in your mind. I dare promise
That you will there find glorious fidelity.]
(My translation)

As we read these lines, what is clear is that the speaker in this fragment is not the 'husband' himself. The speaker is reporting to the addressee in an epistle what a warm welcome he has received from his lord, with whom he is now reunited, after making a journey over the waves. He is writing from where he is now, away from his and his lord's old homestead, where the intended recipient of the epistle still resides. In the ensuing lines the speaker encourages the person who will read the letter to make a journey to where the speaker is now—by guaranteeing that the addressee will also receive a warm welcome from his lord. The 'message' constitutes the major bulk of the poem, or the rest of the fragment. The ensuing thirteen lines read:

Hwæt, þec þonne biddan het se þisne beam agrof
þæt þu sinchroden sylf gemunde
on gewitlocan wordbeotunga,
þe git on ærdagum oft gespræcon,
þenden git moston on meoduburgum
eard weardigan, an lond bugan,
freondscype fremman. Hine fæhþo adraf
of sigeþeode; heht nu sylfa þe
lustum læran, þæt þu lagu drefde,
siþþan þu gehyrde on hliþes oran
galan geomorne geac on bearwe.

Ne læt þu þec siþþan siþes getwæfan,
lade gelettan lifgendne monn. (13-25)

[Look, he, who carved this wood, then ordered me
To implore you, richly adorned, to bring back
The memory of the plights and promises to your mind,
That you two agreed upon in olden days,
While you two could in the mead cities
Occupy an abode, inhabit the same estate,
And openly show your mutual love. A feud drove him away
From his powerful kinsfolk. He himself has ordered me now
To persuade you that you joyfully should stir the sea,
When you have heard from the hillside's edge
The sad cuckoo-bird sings in the grove.
Then allow not any living man to turn you
Away from the journey, or hinder the course.]
(My translation)

One question arises at this point. What a strange way of asking one's wife to come to him—by resorting to the help of an intermediary, who writes down his message for her perusal? Why doesn't the lord personally write to his wife? Why does he need an intermediary? Even if we assume that the speaker has been assigned the mission of sending a message from his lord to his wife, assuring her of a warm welcome, we cannot but suspect the presence of a political concern that keeps the lord from writing to her directly. In the first line quoted above (line 13), we encounter an attention-calling phrase: "se þisne beam agrof" ("he, who carved this wood"). A husband carving on a piece of wood a few letters—runic at that, as they turn out later—that he and his wife, only they, can understand the hidden implication thereof? What a strange way of sending a message to one's wife? Moreover, the lord (or the husband) has ordered the speaker of the lines to implore the addressee to "bring back the memory of the plights and promises to [her] mind. . . ." Why did the unidentified man—whether he is the addressee's husband or not—have to count on a message-writer for persuading the intended addressee to make a journey for reunion with him? Our personal experience is proof enough that, when a man wishes to implore his faraway beloved to embrace all the hardship involved in attaining reunion with him, he will tell her in his own voice—not through an intermediary's! What does all this mean? I suspect that the poem, though in fragment, smacks of a political implication, rather than being a simple message from a loving husband to his wife, urging her to come and join him in sharing a happy life together again.

Scholars have tried to find a link between two Old English fragments—"The Wife's Lament" and "The Husband's Message"— as a mutually corresponding pair of poems, by reading the former as the complaint of a woman alienated from her husband and suffering from the pain of rejection, and the latter as the consolatory words sent from a man to his wife, asking her to make a journey to where he is now in prosperity for a happy reunion. I find it hard to agree with this view. In an essay published years ago, I tried to prove that the speaker of the poem, commonly entitled "The Wife's Lament," is not a woman, but a young retainer that has been alienated from, or ostracized by, the company of the lord that he has served.[1] I argued that the ostensibly female voice in the poem is a metaphor of a young retainer's lament over being an outcast, rather than literally the lament of a woman in dejection.

Now I wish to suggest that the fragment, commonly referred to as "The Husband's Message," may have been wrongfully denominated so. To rush to my conclusion, the fragment could be given a different name, say, "The Refugee Thane's Call of His Beloved Retainer." The voice heard throughout the work is that of a retainer, who has found out, after making a journey to rejoin his lord living in exile, that his lord, who had to leave his clansmen behind on an urgent occasion for some reason 'political' in nature—"a feud drove him away from his powerful kinsfolk" (19b-20a)—is now in

---

1. Sung-Il Lee, "The Identity of the 'Geong Mon' in *The Wife's Lament* (or, *The Lament of an Outcast*)," *Global Perspective on Medieval English Literature, Language, and Culture*, Ed. Noel Harold Kaylor, Jr., and Richard Scott Nokes, Kalamazoo: Medieval Institute, 2007. 175-193.

a situation that may enable him to accommodate his former companions in his new settlement. It is possible that the retainer, who has been reunited with his lord, is sending his lord's message to one of his former companions at home, who has not yet rejoined his lord in refuge. But even if this supposition is reserved for consideration in our reading of the poem, why did he make his letter read like one written for the perusal of his lord's wife, a woman separated from her husband?

> Ongin mere secan, mæwes eþel,
> onsite sænacan, þæt þu suð heonan
> ofer merelade monnan findest,
> þær se þeoden is þin on wenum.
> Ne mæg him worulde willa gelimpan
> mara on gemyndum, þæs þe he me sægde,
> þonne inc geunne alwaldend god
> [. . . . .] ætsomne siþþan motan
> secgum ond gesiþum s[. . . . . . .]
> næglede beagas; he genoh hafað
> fædan gold[.]s [. . . . .
> . . . .]d elþeode eþel healde,
> fægre foldan [. . . . .
> . . . . .]ra hæleþa, þeah þe he her min wine[. . . . .]
> nyde gebæded, nacan ut aþrong,
> ond on yþa geong [. . . . . .] sceolde
> faran on flotweg, forðsiþes georn,
> mengan merestreamas. Nu se mon hafað
> wean oferwunnen; nis him wilna gad,
> ne meara ne maðma ne meododreama,
> ænges ofer eorþan eorlgestreona,
> þeodnes dohtor, gif he þin beneah (26-47)[2]

2. My reading at this point shows slight departure from the punctuation as given in *The Anglo-Saxon Poetic Records*, and follows what was proposed by R. F. Leslie in his *Three Old English Elegies*. The text in the former edition reads:

[Get on your way to seek the sea, the seagull's domain;
Get on board a ship, so that you to the south from here
May find the man when the sea-track is over;
There your prince is waiting for you to arrive.
No greater desire can happen to him in the world
In his mind, according to what he said to me,
Than that the almighty God may grant you two
To be together and afterwards be able to
Distribute treasure, the studded bracelets,
To men and companions. He has enough
Of burnished gold, ...
Throughout the foreign people he holds domain,
Fair earth . . . .
Of devoted men, though here my friend. . . .
Compelled by necessity, pushed out a boat,
And on the expanses of waves alone had to
Voyage on the sea, and eager for departure,
Stir up the sea-currents. Now the man has
Overcome his woes; he does not lack desired things—
Horses, treasures, pleasures in the mead-hall,
Any of the noble treasures on earth,
A prince's daughter—if he owns you.]
(My translation)

---

gif he þin beneah.
ofer eald gebeot incer twega.
Gehyre ic ætsomne. . . . (47b-49a)

R. F. Leslie provides a different punctuation to the lines:
        gif hē þīn beneah.
Ofer eald gebēot incer twēga,
gehyre ic ætsomne. . . . (47b-49a)

In Leslie's reading, there is a full stop after the word 'beneah,' and a new sentence starts with 'Ofer,' whereas in *The Anglo-Saxon Poetic Records* a period is put after the word 'twega.' Also, the word 'Gecyre' in the former edition is being replaced by 'gehyre'—which, I think, makes more sense than 'Gecyre.'

The key words that have led scholars to believe that the intended recipient of the message is unquestionably a woman, possibly the lord's wife or betrothed, are "sinchroden" (14) ("richly adorned") and "þeodnes dohtor, gif he þin beneah" (47) ("a prince's daughter—if he owns you"). 'Sinchroden' is an epithet often used in referring to a woman of high social rank.[3] What I wish to emphasize at this point is that the critical misinterpretation of the whole work arises from taking the apparently feminine addressee literally as the refugee thane's wife. What the speaker emphasizes is that his thane in refuge has now everything necessary for reclaiming his former status as the chieftain of a band of warriors—with enough retainers and wealth that may enable him to re-establish himself as a strong military leader again—except a spouse of royal descent, who may enhance his social status as a true 'ring-giver.' If the addressee joins his camp, after making a journey over the waves, in spite of all the difficulties that may hinder it, then his former lord may become even stronger a commander of warriors, and eventually will act as a true 'ring-giver'—the way Hrothgar was with Wealhtheow as his queen—to extend the metaphor of reunion with his wife to reunion with a retainer, with whom he used to pledge lifelong loyalty and mutual commitment. This is what the line ("a prince's daughter—if he owns you") implies in the guise of appealing to the addressee to fulfill the oath of conjugal fidelity. To repeat what I have said, the message is not directed literally to "a prince's daughter," as scholars have believed, but to a retainer that the thane in refuge, trying to have his former political power restored, wishes to join his newly-built military camp.

When the refugee thane left his home in a hurry, it was due to the impending danger of physical harm: "A feud drove him away / from his powerful kinsfolk" (19b–20a), and "Compelled by necessity, pushed out a boat,/and on the expanses of waves alone had to/ voyage on the sea, and eager for departure,/stir up the

---

3. In *Beowulf*, the epithet 'goldhroden,' similar to 'sinchroden' in meaning and the formation of a single word by combining a noun and the participial suffix '-hroden,' appears several times in referring to Wealhþeow. (*Beowulf*, 616, 640, etc.)

sea-currents" (40–43b). Surely, that kind of situation could have arisen in the course of a fight for political hegemony. And when he ran away to save his life, leaving his wife behind, he must have been well aware that it would be impossible for her to embark on a voyage at will, while being in a strict house-arrest. He cannot be so thoughtless, or so uncaring, as to encourage her to get on her way to join her husband, despite all the risks involved. The retainer who writes the letter may have gotten the idea of addressing his letter to his lord's wife from his lord, or simply decided to do so, on his own. What matters, in view of the given situation, is that even if the letter falls into the hands of his lord's enemies, they would simply take it as a letter bearing a runaway man's longing for his beloved wife, and not suspect any clandestine attempt at reunion going on between their enemy and a man still loyal to him.

If the message was really from a man to his wife, why did he have to ask the message-deliverer to present a piece of wood carved with those enigmatic runic letters, as they appear in the last lines that conclude the message?

> ofer eald gebeot incer twega,
> Gecyre ic ætsomne [two runic inscriptions] geador
> [two runic inscriptions] ond [one runic inscription]
> aþe benemnan,
> þæt he þa wære ond þa winetreowe
> be him lifgendum læstan wolde,
> þe git on ærdagum oft gespræconn. (48–53)

> [Concerning the old promise of you two,
> I hear together S and R sounding at the same time,
> EA, W, and M to declare by oath
> That he would fulfill while being alive
> The pledge and plight of lifelong fidelity,
> Which you two often agreed upon in the days gone.]
> (My translation)

No man, asking his beloved wife to come to him, after spending years building up military power and wealth that may enable

him to attempt to regain the status of a ring-giver, would empha-
size the wealth he has amassed in the meantime, and, furthermore,
include some runic letters in his message to his beloved wife.
When cryptic emblems or codes appear in a message, especially
when it is delivered in the voice of a third person (the one whose
voice is employed throughout the poem), the message should not
be taken simply as a manifestation of simple love-longing. Surely
there is a touch of underlying political implication. The poetic
fragment smacks of a political scheme in action, despite its façade
of a simple imploration for man-and-wife reunion.

We don't have to probe too far into a possibly complex
political entanglement and exert undue imagination to under-
stand what goes on in a poetic fragment. All we have to do is
to read it as it stands, and to interpret it only to the extent of
what it tells us. A man of distinction in a tribe had to leave his
homestead suddenly for some urgent reasons: "A feud drove
him away/ from his powerful kinsfolk" (19b-20a). "Compelled
by necessity, pushed out a boat,/ and on the expanses of waves
alone had to/ voyage on the sea, and eager for departure,/ stir up
the the sea-currents" (40-43a). Now, after spending a number of
years, living in exile and hardship, he has managed to build up
a certain degree of military power and material prosperity in his
newly found domain: "Now the man has/ overcome his woes;
he does not lack desired things—/ horses, treasures, pleasure in
the mead-hall,/ any of the noble treasures on earth,/ a prince's
daughter—if he owns you" (43b-47). The man living in exile has
managed to build up a new power in the place where he lives in
exile, and what he needs now to attain his political ambition is
having his troop reinforced with his former retainers, who still
stay behind at his original homestead.

Charles W. Kennedy, who published a Modern English ver-
sion of Old English poetry more than a half-century ago, trans-
lated 43b-47 as follows:

> Now his troubles are over and all distress,
> He lacks no wealth that the heart may wish,
> Jewels and horses and joys of the hall,

> Nor any fair treasure that earth can afford.
> O Prince's daughter! If he may possess thee. . . .

He punctuated in such a way that "þeodnes dohtor" is being treated as in the vocative case; accordingly, he read the message as an infallibly personal one from the refugee lord to his wife. No wonder scholars have unanimously shared the notion that the addressee in the fragment is a woman—the refugee lord's wife—rather than a former retainer of his, who is left behind at his old homestead, and whom the lord ardently wishes to make a journey over the waves for reunion. The old pledges and plights between the lord and his beloved retainer (the addressee) are repeatedly invoked for the sake of remembrance. The whole poetic fragment is an unidentified refugee thane's message to his beloved retainer strongly tied to him by the oaths of *comitatus*.

A word on the poetic subgenre the fragment may be allocated to. R. F. Leslie classified *The Husband's Message* as an 'elegy.' 'Elegy' means a work that laments the death of a person, or making an utterance over the general human misery categorically. But can we apply the term 'elegy' in defining the character of the work? I doubt it. There is not the tone and mood in the fragment that may justify the use of the term, 'elegy' or 'elegiac.' The epistle supposedly written by a retainer to his lord's wife (at least on the surface level) reads more like a message from a political schemer (loyal to his lord) to his pal, whom he wishes very much to join his camp for his lord's triumphant return to his old homestead as the final winner in the tribal feud.

The Old English poetic fragment universally referred to as "The Husband's Message" has been interpreted simply as the message that a lord living in exile sends to his wife or betrothed, asking her to make a journey across the sea for familial reunion. The message is being delivered in the voice of a retainer, who has recently attained reunion with his lord by crossing the sea. The appearance of the words denoting femininity—"sinchroden" and "þeodnes dohtor"—in reference to the addressee notwithstanding, the fact that the whole message is being delivered by an intermediary, whose voice is employed throughout the fragment, indicates that the message should not be read only on its surface level. I argue that the husband-to-wife message is only a façade, a frame set for covering a political implication of the work—an exiled lord urging a former retainer of his to come and join his newly built camp. A political situation involving the reinforcement of one's military power in preparation for an upcoming feudal strife necessitates the deceptive frame of a husband sending his message to his wife or betrothed. There is nothing 'elegiac' in the fragment, and no romantic longing for one's farawy spouse. Only the exiled lord's desire to have his camp reinforced with the help of a retainer he had to leave behind at his old homestead.

A Note on the Translator

SUNG-IL LEE EARNED HIS M. A. at University of California, Davis, in March, 1973, and Ph. D. at Texas Tech University in December, 1980. He was appointed an Assistant Professor of Englsih at Yonsei University, Seoul, in March, 1981. Having taught at Yonsei University for twenty-eight years, he retired to be nominated Professor Emeritus of English Language and Literature in February, 2009.

His major publication in the field of Medieval English literature includes *Beowulf in Parallel Texts* (Cascade Books, 2017), a book containing his Modern English verse translation of the Old English epic. The late Robert D. Stevick, who wrote a Foreword for this translation of *Beowulf*, concludes his observation:

> Forty-five years since I began leading others through the labyrinth of diction, variation, narrative embellishments of *Beowulf*, and reading their translation examinations, and reading most of the published translations, and forty years since I began scrutiny of the spellings and grapho-tactics system of the sole manuscript text. When I carefully read this new translation line by line, making notes on the many surprising but always interesting locutions, the movement forward was felt all the way through, with even the episodes and digressions (as they are usually regarded) seeming to be at first unproblematic, and then appearing, as they should, as beautiful assets to the action-narrative and its affectivity. In brief, the translation

by Dr. Sung-Il Lee succeeded better for an old reader (that I am) than earlier ones have done, and my sense is that it will succeed very well for readers with any degree of less familiarity with the earliest known text. If we still offered seminars on The Art of Translation, this would be a good centerpiece. An old poem here, unimpaired in translation. It is the best we have among the remnants of Anglo-Saxon culture, and in its newer voice.